Anonymous

Madagascar

Its mission and its martyrs

Anonymous

Madagascar
Its mission and its martyrs

ISBN/EAN: 9783337318482

Printed in Europe, USA, Canada, Australia, Japan

Cover: Foto ©Andreas Hilbeck / pixelio.de

More available books at **www.hansebooks.com**

MADAGASCAR:

ITS MISSION AND ITS MARTYRS.

FIFTH THOUSAND.

LONDON:

JOHN SNOW, 35, PATERNOSTER ROW.

MDCCCLXIII.

PREFACE.

———————

In many parts of the World, the great Head of the Church has honoured the operations of the London Missionary Society with large success, but nowhere more signally than in Madagascar. Its Missionaries, indeed, during their fifteen years of labour in that island, could do little more than begin the spiritual house which, since then, has been growing "unto an holy temple in the Lord." But what they did was done well. They built upon a rock; and, so far as they saw the superstructure rise, it largely consisted of "gold, silver, and precious stones," such as, when "revealed by fire," would "abide." This, to use the words of the Bishop of Mauritius, was "the noble work of the London Missionary Society—a work which has stood the test of long years of fiery persecution, and has left results full of promise for the future." "I think I may say with truth," he added, at a recent meeting of the Auxiliary Bible Society in that island, "that I was never more impressed in my life with anything, than I was at witnessing the results occasioned by the spread of Christian truth in Madagascar. It is my firm opinion that it is impossible for any one to feel the full force of this impression, unless he has witnessed and studied it himself. The effect of Christian teaching in Madagascar struck me as possessing a most remarkable character."

Of this work the present volume contains an outline, with numerous incidents, which strikingly indicate its Divine origin. More than this it would have been unwise to attempt, within limits so restricted. The documents and details which belong to the history of the first twenty years of the Mission, must therefore be sought in the admirable works of the Rev. W. Ellis, and Messrs. Freeman and Johns. But although the following pages contain merely a concise sketch of the progress and effects of Christianity in Madagascar during the protracted period of persecution now so happily terminated, it is believed that such a narrative is urgently required; that, considering the previous condition of those

whose faith and patience it describes, more marvellous illustrations of the operation of " the word
of truth " and " the power of God " are not to be
found in the history of the Church ; and that no
Christians present a stronger claim to confidence
and love, and no Mission more deserves generous
support.

E. PROUT.

Mission House, Blomfield Street,
November, 1862.

MADAGASCAR:

ITS MISSION AND ITS MARTYRS.

UNTIL within a comparatively recent period, few coun-
tries of equal extent and importance have attracted less attention or awakened less interest than Madagascar. With
an area larger than that of Great Britain and Ireland
combined; unusually rich in mineral treasures and vege-
table productions; fitted by its position, climate, soil, and
harbours, to become wealthy and powerful; and capable,
moreover, of supporting a population manyfold greater than
the four millions by which it is now inhabited, this fine
island would have been scarcely missed from the map of the
globe, had its name been expunged at the beginning of
the present century. But forty years ago, Philanthropists
and Christians hailed with gladness the commencement of
a new era in its history; and bright indeed did that
era promise to become. Its dawn was as a morning without clouds. But, alas! it proved as brief as it was bright.
Portentous darkness soon followed, and at length a storm
burst, which for nearly thirty years desolated the land.
Great indeed was the grief of those who had laboured for
the salvation of its inhabitants, when, driven from its

shores, they heard from afar the wail of sorrow and the cry for help. And the pain thus produced became more acute as years rolled on, and fragments of intelligence —at long intervals—reached them, which revealed the character of the sufferers and the extent of their sufferings. Christian sympathy had place in many hearts, and the prayer arose from many lips, "Lord, how long shall the wicked triumph?" And once and again it was believed that that prayer had been heard. The clouds seemed to open, and gleams of brightness to break through them. But they "returned after the rain." Hope, thus long deferred, and often disappointed, made the heart sick. Supplications, indeed, were still made to God continually, and many a weary watcher looked out with sad and sorrowful thoughts upon the darkness, and longed for day. Thanks be to God! the day has at length dawned—and that, too, with no hazy indistinctness, no shadowy forebodings of another storm. And, what should add to the joy with which we mark the change, is the fact now so clearly revealed, that, while the darkness prevailed, the sun above it was not merely shining on, but rising higher, and attaining the lofty altitude from which he is now flooding hill and valley, city and village, with beams far brighter than those of his early rising. These changes it is the object of the following pages very briefly to describe.

The history of the Madagascar Mission is comprehended within a period of rather more than forty years. It dates from 1820, when Missionaries from the London Missionary Society commenced their labours at Antananarivo, the capital. The necessity for such a movement had been felt by the Directors for many years. Early in the present century, they had requested Dr. Vanderkemp, then in South Africa, whose heart was set upon the service, to visit the island with that intent. But this he was unable to do, and it was not until 1814 that a Missionary was stationed at Mauritius, chiefly for the purpose of obtaining information and adopting measures with a view to the establishment of a Mission in Madagascar. The result was, that in the autumn of 1818, Messrs. Bevan and Jones commenced their labours at Tamatave. But the climate of the country was then imperfectly understood. The devoted Brethren knew but little of the deadly malaria which during the rainy season surrounded the coast, and their ignorance proved most fatal. In a short time, malignant fever had consigned Mr. and Mrs. Bevan, Mrs. Jones and two children to the grave, while Mr. Jones, with broken health and bleeding heart, was compelled to return to Mauritius.

Taught wisdom by this most painful experience, Mr. Jones, on his return to Madagascar, proceeded forthwith to Antananarivo, the capital, which occupies a high and healthy position in the centre of the island. Other labourers, several of them artizans, speedily followed, and entered with energy and hope upon their work. But their early difficulties were great. They had everything to learn and everything to teach. The people, though slightly acquainted with a few mechanical arts, had no written language. The first Missionaries had therefore to learn by the ear alone, and to catch and record as they best could, the unfamiliar and uncouth words and phrases which came rushing from the lips of the natives. For some time, their labours were almost necessarily confined to the schools and the children; but as, hitherto, the Malagasy knew little of Europeans, except as slave-dealers, many of the parents regarded the proceedings of the Missionaries with suspicion, not un-mixed with fear for the safety of their little ones. The King, however, Radama I., early discerned the secular advantages which he and his people would derive from their instructions, and from the first he gave them his countenance and aid. He sent the sons of his highest nobles to be taught, and took a pleasure in visting the school, to hear them recite their lessons and sing their hymns. Soon the children became attached to their teachers and to the school, to many of whom the daily task was only a most pleasant occupation. Often, indeed, before daybreak, as if impatient to begin their work, would groups of them gather outside the teacher's house, repeating the multiplication table, or other prescribed exercises in which they were interested. An unexpected and amusing proof of their fondness for the school oc-curred a short time after its commencement. Wanting some relaxation for themselves, and imagining that Mala-gasy children, like boys and girls at home, would be gratified with a holiday, one day the announcement was made that the school would be closed for a short time. This was a surprise and a mystery to the parents, and the only ex-planation they could imagine was, that the Missionaries intended in this way to punish their children for some unknown offence. A *kabary*, or public council, was con-sequently summoned to investigate the matter, and even the King sent to inquire what the children had done. Of course the explanation was as satisfactory to the parents, as their anxiety for the improvement of the children was encouraging to the Missionaries.

But although, at first, before native assistants had been trained, the Missionaries were compelled to devote much of their attention to the schools, no opportunity was lost, either by them or by the Christian artizans, for teaching and preaching the Gospel. As soon, moreover, as they had acquired some familiarity with the language, they began a translation of the Scriptures, and the preparation of other works of instruction ; and when, after some years, printing-presses were set up, the wonder and delight of the people were almost unbounded. The rapidity with which the young, and those adults who had felt anything of the influence of religion, learned to read, caused a demand for books far beyond the supply. This was especially the case with the Scriptures, the desire to possess which was very strong. Of this, a single illustration must suffice. Two young persons came to the Missionary, one of whom, a respectable female, had a slate in her hand, which she presented to him, with the following note written upon it :—

" I have long lived in darkness, and now desire to be brought into the light, that I may know about God, and his Son Jesus Christ. Oh! pity me! Have compassion upon me! Give me a copy of the New Testament! I am greatly in need of it. Be merciful to me, and grant me my request, if you possibly can!"

The increasing supply of books, now of all treasures the most precious in the estimation of many, proved not only a satisfaction to those who could read, but a strong stimulus to others to follow their example. Thus the demand for instruction spread, and the number of schools, both in the capital and in the country, increased so rapidly, that a general superintendence of them was all the Missionaries could give ; and, happily, more was not necessary. Many of the young people had by this time become qualified to teach others ; and fortunate were they esteemed, who were elevated to this service. Thus, when a new school was opened, many eager candidates competed for the appointment of teacher ; and though these were not always Christians in the highest sense, they were familiar with the Scriptures, and had learned to despise the idols and superstitions of their country.

The effect of the education thus wide-spread, was soon apparent. The taught imbibed the sentiments and manifested the spirit of the teachers. It was inevitable that a change so great should provoke resentment and resistance. One day, the headman of a village, in which stood the shrine of a popular idol, heard that the teacher had spoken of it with contempt. In a great rage, the petty chieftain hurried off to the school, and charged the young man with the crime. The teacher at once acknowledged it, adding that the idol was nothing, and of less use than the mere dust of the ground. A heavy blow from the heathen was the only answer which the brave youth received. Nor were the children much more respectful to the gods than their instructors. In one place, a hailstorm had damaged the crops. This, the heathen attributed to the insults offered by the children to the deities, and which they threatened to avenge, unless they were treated with greater reverence. But, as young Madagascar was not to be scared and silenced by hard words and angry blows, their parents spoke of complaining to the King, and added with sorrow, "We have nursed you, and brought you up until this day; but now you forsake the customs of your forefathers." "We cannot," replied the children, "prevent your complaining to the King, but we have been taught to tell the truth; and if, to please you, we should say with our lips that we believe in the idol, while yet in our hearts we cannot do so, we should only lie." In despair of bringing back their children to the point from which they had now drifted far away, by any influence of their own, the parents went to Radama, and in tones of bitter complaint cried, "Our children are forsaking the customs of our ancestors, and our gods," ascribing the change to the schools. But the King was too wise to interpose. So he quietly dismissed them with the admonition, "Do you mind your work, and the children mind their lessons."

But the Missionaries were concerned that both teacher and taught should not only possess "the form of knowledge and of truth," but that they should feel its power. With this view they held meetings for special prayer, which many of the young regularly attended, and in which some of them took a public part, pouring out, in simple but earnest petitions, desires which the Missionaries believed God had inspired in their hearts.

As this volume is not designed to furnish a circumstantial narrative of the origin of the Madagascar Mission, or of its early progress, we shall merely add that, at the end of eight years from the settlement of Mr. Jones at Antananarivo, there were four thousand young people under Christian instruction, many of them children of the most powerful nobles in the land, some of whom subsequently brought forth the ripened fruits of the cultivation they now received.

But while education was thus spreading, large congregations statedly listened to the Gospel; Bible Classes were formed, a Church was gathered, a considerable portion of the Scriptures, with many Christian books, was printed, and a feeling in favour of the new religion had spread far, and was constantly spreading farther in the city and through the surrounding province of Imerina.

Up to this point of their history, therefore, there was much of the bright and the fair in the prospects of the Missionaries. Nevertheless, their sky had been far from cloudless. Many occurrences had caused grief, and awakened anxiety. Once and again death had visited their little circle. The King, though their friend, and favourable to many of their proceedings, had no sympathy with their spiritual design; and although he cared but little for the idols, he appeared to care still less for the Gospel. He moreover delighted in war, and when provoked, could show how much of the savage there was still in him. The people, too, were mostly heathen. These and other discouragements moderated the joy with which they reaped the first fruits of their labour, and surveyed on every side the early signs of a far larger ingathering.

But at the time of which we write (1828) Radama died, when he was only thirty-six years of age. The Missionaries felt the loss to be that of a protector and friend. But as yet they had no dark forebodings of the future. The rightful heir to the vacant throne was an excellent youth, named Rakotobe, who had been their first pupil, and in whose heart they believed there was some good thing to-

ANTANANARIVO, THE CAPITAL OF MADAGASCAR.

wards the Lord God of Israel. Under his government
they knew that their labours would have the widest scope,
and the most enlightened encouragement. Rakotobe's
father's name was Rataffe. This prince visited England
in 1821, and was a mild and excellent man. The mother,
too, of Rakotobe was Radama's eldest sister. Nobody,
therefore, could question his title to the throne, and it was
generally expected that he would succeed to it in peace.
But this was not to be.

Radama had twelve wives. None of these were entitled
to reign; but one of them, Ranavalona, resolved to
grasp the sceptre as it fell from Radama's hand. She was
a bold, bad woman, with strong purpose and no principle.
Though well aware that she could only gain her object by
crime, she was ready to dare and to do the worst. With
this view she drew a few men, as reckless and as wicked as
herself into the plot, promising, no doubt, high offices and
large rewards as the recompense of their villainy. But how
could she attain the desired eminence? Murder was the
sole means. The throne could only be reached over the
slaughtered bodies of the rightful heir and his loyal adherents. But for all this she was prepared. Her first victim
was Rakotobe. Violent and armed men hurried from her
presence and seized him, ere the shadow of coming danger
had fallen upon his path. And as if death were not all that
the murderess desired, the cruel instruments of her ambition dug the prince's grave before his eyes. While they
were thus engaged, the pious youth kneeled down to pray,
and in that attitude was pierced by the executioners'
spears. Immediately afterwards, his father and mother
met the same fate; but the Queen had commanded that

the latter should be starved to death. A similar order was executed upon Ratafikia, Radama's brother, who lingered in agony eight days. Then Rakatobe's grandmother and other relations were cut down by her ruthless hand, until all had been destroyed who were likely to oppose her usurpation. Thus did Ranavalona become Queen of Madagascar. It was a beginning which agreed but too well with her long reign of darkness and terror, tyranny, persecution, and crime. Of this we shall meet with too many appalling details as we proceed—details which would have no place here but for the fact that side by side with them, and in contrast with the usurper's deeds of cruelty and blood, stand forth a glorious array of Christian confessors and martyrs, together with evidences of the progress and the power of the religion for which they suffered, few parallels to which will be found in the history of the Church. In that contrast we shall see, as we proceed with our wondrous tale, one reason, at least, why He who sitteth in the heavens permitted the heathen to rage, and this sanguinary ruler to imagine so vain a thing against the Lord and against his Anointed, as to say, "Let us break their bonds asunder, and cast away their cords from us."

The feelings of the Missionaries, when they heard that Ranavalona reigned, and became aware of the means by which she had attained power, may be imagined. At first, however, they were not alarmed for their converts, or for the cause they were promoting. They knew, indeed, that the Queen was a besotted devotee of idolatry, and that priests, and sorcerers, and diviners would have her patronage and favour ; nor were they unaware of the fact that the men whose bloodstained hands had lifted her to the throne, and who would support her there, were as bigoted as she. Still, they hoped for the best, and laboured on; and as, for some time after Radama's death, they were not hindered in their work, they trusted that all would continue to go on well. Nevertheless, they knew that the will of such a woman was a false and precarious ground of confidence. They therefore laboured more abundantly than before, in teaching, preaching, translating, and printing, that, should their worst fears be realized, the fruit of their toil might not only with God's blessing abound, but abide. And no doubt but that He who sees the end from the beginning, put this purpose into their hearts, and gave them a more than ordinary measure of strength and skill for its efficient accomplishment; for seldom have labours such as theirs proved more necessary, or more productive of spiritual results.

In order to allay the fears of the friends of social progress and Christianity, Ranavalona, shortly after being proclaimed Queen, sent to inform the Missionaries that it was her purpose to tread in the footsteps of Radama; and not long after this, in a more public form, she solemnly engaged to carry out his plans for the education and improvement of the people. But while thus acting, her desire to sustain the reputation of the idols, to perpetuate the customs of her ancestors, and to destroy the rapidly extending influence of the Europeans, could not be disguised. There was, however, a formidable obstacle on the threshold of that course of repression and violence by which her reign was subsequently characterized. At that time, her chief nobles and advisers formed two opposing parties. One of these was

headed by a young officer named Andriamihaja, a great
favourite of the Queen, and a friend of the Missionaries;
the other was led by two brothers—Rainiharo and Rain-
imaharo, the former being the guardian of one of the chief
idols, and both of them determined enemies to the Christians. For two years, the party of Andriamihaja was
strong enough to prevent the retrograde movement which
his rivals and the Queen desired; but at length the ido-
latrous party prevailed. While in a state of intoxication,
they procured from Ranavalona the death-warrant of Andriamihaja, who was immediately afterwards murdered in
his own house.

Thus one formidable barrier was removed out of the
path which the heathen party were anxious to take. Happily, however, the two years in which these factions had
been contending for supremacy, were well improved by the
Missionaries, who laboured with increased energy and great
success in preparing books and teaching the people. Contrary to their expectations, no material change appeared in
the conduct of the Queen; and even so late as the spring of
1831, she permitted her subjects to be baptized, and repeated her declaration that she would not "change the
words of the King."

It was not long, however, before premonitory symptoms
of approaching evil appeared. One of the first of these
was an intimation to some Christian officers of the Government, who were about to join the Church in the capital,
that their so doing would be displeasing to their royal
mistress. This was soon followed by a proclamation, pro-
hibiting the soldiers, and those whom the Government had
placed in the schools, from being baptized, or receiving the

Lord's Supper. By the close of the same year (1831) a similar prohibition was extended to the people at large. Happily, no restrictions had as yet been put upon the liberty of the Missionaries to preach or print. In these departments, therefore, they continued to labour, if possible, more abundantly than ever. And at this time God gave testimony to the word of His grace. The congregations were large, and a spirit of thoughtfulness and devotion appeared to pervade them. The readers, too, had multiplied by thousands, and the press was scattering Christian books through the land. But, as it was obvious that the schools were only tolerated because some useful arts were taught in them, the Missionaries were not surprised when at length an order appeared that no slave was any longer to attend them.

About the same time, the Rev. D. Griffiths was commanded to leave the country, and shortly afterwards two other Missionaries were required to follow him. Thus new links were being added to the iron chain of despotic power which the Missionaries saw was continually drawn closer around the now narrow sphere of their operations. Still, the process was slow, and even up to the beginning of the year 1835, there had been no interference with public worship. At no previous period had the sanctuaries been so crowded, while there were few families, from those most nearly related to the Queen down to the households of the slaves, in which disciples of the Saviour could not be found. But at last the crisis came. No very powerful incitement was required to transform the latent hatred of the sovereign and her councillors into active hostility against the Christians. This was now furnished. One Sabbath in February, as she was carried in her state palanquin through the city, Ranavalona passed a chapel while the congregation was singing, and immediately remarked to her attendants, " They will not stop till some of them lose their heads."

Soon after this she was told that many of the Christians, and amongst them a near connection of one of her chief ministers, had spoken disrespectfully of the idols. About the same time another incident came to her knowledge, which fanned the flame of her anger. A young man, who, during his residence in the capital, had become a Christian, while visiting some friends in a village where an idol was kept, ventured, rather freely, to express his surprise that any person could be so ignorant as to trust a useless log of wood; and his offence was aggravated by the fact that he would not swear, nor work on the Sabbath, and that at night he drew the people to meet with him for prayer. These crimes were charged before the judge, and by him were reported to the Queen. That the guilt or innocence of the accused might appear, he was required to drink the tangena —the poison-water ordeal. The Christians trembled for their friend, but they also prayed, and God heard them. To express their joy at his deliverance, many residing in the capital imprudently marched in procession through the streets. This was reported to the Queen, and increased her anger. Just then a chief of rank and influence having obtained admission to her presence, thus addressed her, " I am come to ask your Majesty for a spear—a bright and sharp spear—grant my request." Being asked for what purpose he wanted the weapon, his answer was, that the idols—the guardians of the land—were dishonoured; that

the hearts of the people were turned from the customs of
their ancestors; that by their teaching and their books the
Missionaries had drawn away many nobles and officers of
the army, as well as people of the inferior orders; and that
ruin would come upon the land unless these evils were
speedily stopped; and " as," he added, " such will be the
issue of the teaching of the foreigners, and as I do not wish
to see that calamity come upon my country, I ask for a
spear, to pierce my heart before the evil day comes." This
appeal produced its designed effect.   Greatly moved with
grief and rage, the Queen first wept, then sat in silence for
about half an hour, and at length solemnly declared that
she would put an end to Christianity, if it cost the life of
every Christian in her land.   Her councillors and attendants fully apprehended the fearful import of her tearful
silence and terrible threat.   They were the meet precursors
of that outburst of vengeance which so soon, and for so
long a period, desolated Madagascar.   The following fortnight was strongly marked by evil omens.   All that time
profound silence prevailed within the palace.   Music,
dancing, and all kinds of amusement were intermitted.
The court appeared as if mourning for some dreadful
disaster or death; and as the intelligence spread amongst
·the people, it filled a multitude of hearts with faintness
and fear.

No time was lost in carrying out the royal threatening.   Only a few days after its utterance, as the Missionaries were proceeding to their Thursday evening
service, they received a summons to hear that message
from the Queen which put a final stop to all their public
labours.

On the 1st of March the people were summoned to a great assembly convened to hear the royal prohibition of Christianity, together with a command that all Christians should confess their crime within a month,* or suffer death. The day of trial and the reign of terror had now commenced.

During the following week, multitudes confessed that they had read Christian books, and attended Christian worship, acknowledging their crime and submitting themselves to the royal pleasure. But there were others who disregarded the Queen's commands; and this they did, well knowing the consequences of refusal, but resolved to suffer rather than sin. That they might be able to act thus, prayer was made unto God; and never with more freedom or fervour than during that anxious week.

Let us in thought visit one or two of the hallowed spots where the Christians now met to commune with each other, and with their common Lord. It is midnight. The darkness and silence are unbroken. No voice nor footstep is heard in the streets of the capital. But here and there, individuals might have been discerned silently stealing along under the deep shadows of the houses. All these are bending their steps towards one point—the house of prayer. Let us follow them, as they enter the place where God had often met and blessed them. A smile of loving recognition glances from face to face, tempered with a shade of sadness and anxiety. They join in prayer; but in the midst of their devotions a stranger enters. He is an officer of high rank in the army, is an honourable and friendly man, but not hitherto known as a Christian. Filled with surprise, not

* By a subsequent order restricted to a week.

unmixed with apprehension, the brethren suspend the
service, and wait in silence for an explanation. This is
frankly given. The officer declares himself to be one of
their number, and that he had been constrained to join them,
in this the hour of their weakness and peril, because he
abhorred the injustice with which they had been treated by
the Queen, and the cowardice with which the half-heart-
ed had quailed before her uplifted arm. That was a
memorable night in the history and experience of the
Christians. He who thus, when others shrunk away,
came bravely forth to share their perils, not fearing the
wrath of the Queen, proved subsequently one of their
wisest counsellors, and best protectors. Soon, too, his
wife followed his example, and, with her husband, suc-
coured very many. Such an accession to their number
at such a season, was singularly calculated to confirm the
faith and revive the courage of the little flock, and to
enable them calmly to wait the outburst of the lowering
tempest. But this was not all. These meetings proved,
in an unusual degree, " times of refreshing from the
presence of the Lord," and of gracious preparation for the
fiery trial which was to try them. Long were the midnight
hours of that memorable week remembered as amongst the
brightest and most blissful of their history :—hours, the
sweet influence of which proved in after days a solace and
a support, when, separated from one another, these brethren
beloved were working in chains, or concealed in forests, or
immured in prisons, or anticipating a martyr's death.

But let us now enter another house in the capital, during
the same days of dark expectation. Again it is night.
A few women are gathered within that dwelling. Their

countenances betoken an anxiety which too well agrees with their communications. They are conversing about the edict of the Queen, and the punishments denounced against those who disregard it. Sad and disheartened, just as they are expressing to one another a fear lest their faith should fail in the hour of trial, an unexpected visitor enters. He was no stranger, but a Christian friend from a distant district. And soon it appeared that he had come there with a message from God. Delighted to see him, and assured of his sympathy, the women disclosed their depression and fear. " Have you read God's Word to-day?" he inquired. They told him that, in conse- quence of the confusion, they had been unable to do so. " Have you, then," he continued, " wrestled with God in prayer?" They replied that they had tried to give them- selves up to Him, but that they had been overcome by terror. " I wonder not at this," said the friend. " Let us read the 46th Psalm." With much feeling and solemnity he then proceeded. " God is our refuge and strength ; a very present help in trouble. Therefore will not we fear," &c. After this they kneeled down together, this Christian man conducting their devotions. The sacred exercise brought with it new life and strength. From that hour, the trembling women became courageous ; and long afterwards, some of them declared that, whenever anxious thoughts threw a gloomy shadow upon their path, they scattered them by again reading the 46th Psalm.

The dreary days of that dreadful week were now num- bered ; and another kabary was summoned, at which it was known that the sentences of the Christians would be declared. A large multitude was collected when the judges appeared, holding in their hands the Queen's decree. It began by assuring the Christians that their crimes deserved death, and that, had not the people of the province (Imerina) interceded for them, she would have driven them all down the river and over the cataract. Punishments would therefore be awarded which were far lighter than their deserts. The sentences were then read, which deprived four hundred officers and nobles of their honours, and levied fines upon the remainder, who numbered about two thousand.

This award was followed by another royal mandate, which required all books to be delivered up to the officers, and threatened death against any who kept back, or hid even a single leaf. But like other persecutors, this besotted woman in her blind fury would fain have rivetted her fetters upon the souls of her subjects. With a mad infatuation which provokes a smile, she asserted the right and the power to restrain the free exercise of the mind, and commanded her subjects never again even to think upon the Christian lessons they had learned, but to blot them from their memories for ever !

Amongst the important services which the Missionaries rendered to the Christian cause, in the interval between the suppression of public worship and their departure from the capital, there was one which, in the times of trial now impending, proved inestimable. This was the translation of the "Pilgrim's Progress." Eight copies were transcribed by the Christians for their use in common. And well did they study and wisely apply the teachings of that noble allegory. Often, amidst their wanderings, did its scenes and sayings recur to their memories, and cheer their hearts. Next to the Bible, this was the book which the persecuted Malagasy most prized. One copy, we are told, was found upon a Christian when he was apprehended, and was carefully scrutinized by the Queen's officers; but after vainly attempting to discover its import, they abandoned the task in despair.

But valuable as this service was to the Christians, there was another rendered by the Missionaries at this time, of far higher importance—the completion of the printing of the Scriptures in the Malagasy language. The native printers, indeed, were forbidden to aid in this or any other work connected with the Mission, but yet, with strange inconsistency, the Queen permitted Mr. Baker and other Missionaries to remain in the capital, though she most probably knew that they were preparing and printing prohibited books. It was a happy oversight, and one which went far to neutralize her subsequent endeavours to uproot Christianity from the land.

The Christians also partook of the Lord's Supper together in secret, and not a few, even during this time of terror, were added to their number. Some, fearing that after their teachers had left it would be impossible to procure the Word of God, travelled as far as a hundred miles for a copy. One poor man, who had been confined to his house by illness for many months, nevertheless walked sixty miles to make this much-coveted treasure his own, and when the Missionary placed a Bible in his hand, his countenance became radiant with joy; he pressed the sacred volume to his bosom, and said, " This contains the words of eternal life; it is my life, and I will take as much care of it as of my own life !" And he did as he had said; though driven from his

home and compelled to hide himself in the forests, he proved
faithful unto death.

At length, in 1835, it became but too obvious that the
labours of the Missionaries in Madagascar must terminate.
Most of them, therefore, left the capital during that year.
Messrs. Johns and Baker lingered until the following summer, when, with heavy hearts, they turned from the scenes
of labour which had yielded much and promised more, and
pressed the warm hands of many whom they were leaving
as sheep in the midst of wolves, and whose faces they would
see no more.   Well aware of the existence of many of the
much hated sect, in spite of her edicts and punishments, and
yet unable to convict them, the rage of the Queen continued
to increase.   At the same time, the Christians were becoming better known to one another, and they all did what they
could to encourage themselves and each other in the Lord.
For this purpose they held many secret meetings, sometimes
in solitary houses or upon the summits of mountains, or in
other lonely spots, where they could not only read God's
Word and pray, but engage in the, to them, sweet and
sacred exercise of vocal praise.   And as they now possessed
seventy copies of the entire Scriptures, with a still larger
number of New Testaments, Psalms, and Christian books,
which were always carefully concealed and often buried in
the ground, until wanted for use, they had in their hands
means of instruction and consolation which they knew well
how to employ.

Amongst the most devoted of this Christian band was
the well-remembered Rafaravavy.   Prior to her conversion
she had been a zealous upholder of idolatry, but from
the time her heart was given to the Saviour, she conse-

crated her property, influence, and energy to His service.
At length she was accused by three of her slaves of at-
tending religious meetings.   On hearing of her accusation,
the Queen exclaimed, " Is it possible that there is one so
daring as to defy me !   Go and put her at once to death."
But the intercession of friends, and the former services
of her father, induced the Queen to commute the sentence
into a heavy fine.

The calm, firm, heroic, and yet gentle bearing of this
noble Christian lady, both at this trying period and subsequently while pursuing the path of duty, surrounded by
perils, and in the near view of martyrdom, has rarely been
equalled, and never surpassed.   "I shall never forget,"
wrote Mr. Johns, "the serenity and composure she dis-
played while she related to me the consolations she enjoyed
in pleading the promises and in drawing near to God in
prayer."   It is not surprising that the spirit and conduct
of such a woman should greatly comfort and confirm her
fellow-sufferers.

For some months after the departure of the Missionaries,
the Christians enjoyed comparative peace.   This appears
to have arisen from a persuasion on the part of their oppressors that, when thus left to themselves, they would
soon return to their former practices.   Instead of this,
however, all the letters forwarded to their exiled friends
indicated that the joy of the Lord was their strength, that
some who had drawn back were restored, and that their
number was on the increase.   One valued and honoured
man, indeed, had been taken from them, but his holy life,
closed by a truly Christian death, tended to strengthen the
faith and animate the hopes of the survivors.   They desig-

nate him "a beloved brother," and speak of the great
delight and benefit which they derived from his society.
He was a young man, and remarkable for the depth and
tenderness of his love to the Divine Redeemer. Both
Missionaries and Christians were struck with the circumstance that, whenever he named the name of Jesus, it
brought tears to his eyes, and when he was asked the reason of this, his simple answer was "How can I do other-
wise than feel, while I mention the name of that beloved
Saviour, who suffered and died on the cross for me?" As
the hour of his departure drew near, a Christian brother
inquired whether he had any fear of death. " Why should
I fear to die," he exclaimed, " while Jesus is my friend?
He hath loved me with an everlasting love, and I love Him
because He hath first loved me. I am persuaded that He
will not leave me now, for I am full of joy at the thought of
leaving this sinful world to be for ever with my Saviour."

But the diligence with which the faithful brethren had
improved this brief remission of severe punishment, and
the consequent increase both of the number and influence
of the Christians in the capital, had been so contrary to
the calculations of their enemies, that the Queen and her
counsellors resolved to adopt more severe measures for
their repression. This change first appeared in an accusation which was lodged against fourteen Christians, ten of
whom were apprehended and condemned to perpetual
slavery. One of these was Rafaravavy, whose house was
razed, and her property seized, by an order from the Queen.
At the same time she was chained and imprisoned, and
condemned to be executed on the following morning. But
during the previous night, a fire broke out in the capital,

which aroused the superstitious fears of Ranavalona, and saved Rafaravavy's life. Thus the honour of being the proto-martyr of Madagascar was reserved for another. Amongst the ten who were now imprisoned, was a young woman named Rasalama. While under confinement, she was overheard to express her astonishment that she and her Christian friends should receive such treatment, and then added with much warmth, " When the Tsitialaingia came to my house, I was not afraid, but rather rejoiced that I was counted worthy to suffer affliction for believing in Jesus." This utterance having been reported to the judges, she was ordered to be put into heavy irons and severely beaten ; but throughout these sufferings, so long as she had strength, she sought comfort in singing her favourite hymns. Her firmness and fortitude confounded her persecutors and astonished the people ; and the only solution of the mystery which they could imagine, was that she was under the influence of some very powerful charm. There were those, however, who looked at her calm countenance, and listened to her triumphal words, with far different thoughts and feelings.

During the afternoon preceding the day of her execution, the ordinary chains she wore were exchanged for others, consisting of rings and bars fastened around her hands, feet, knees, and neck, so as to force the body into a position which caused great agony. This was its intended effect. It was done, not for security, but simply for punishment. Joyful, therefore, was she as the time drew on when she would be rescued for ever from the tyrant's power. Seldom has the dawning of day proved more reviving to the sick and the sorrowful than when it came to

Rasalama. To her it was the hour of release and redemption. As she was led away she continued to sing, and thus set an example to be followed afterwards by many who were called to tread the same pathway to death and heaven. When passing the sanctuary in which she had been accustomed to worship, she exclaimed, "There I heard the words of the Saviour!" Though many sympathised with Rasalama, and earnest prayers were offered on her behalf by Christian friends, they knew that, by identifying themselves with her, the little aid they could render her would be at the peril of their own lives. But there was one who could not be restrained by prudential considerations. He was a young man, who, as it appeared, possessed her spirit, and was prepared to follow in her footsteps; his name was Rafaralahy. Fearless of consequences, and pressing through the guard of soldiers by whom Rasalama was surrounded, he walked as near to her side as he could, and said to her, " My sister, I will not leave you till the end!" At length the gl omy procession reached the spot where this Christian woman was to suffer. The name of it is *Ambohipotsy*. It forms the southern extremity of the crest of the hill upon which the city stands.

When Mr. Ellis and the Bishop of Mauritius lately visited it, they saw there the remains of the broken cross, upon which many had hung in anguish, and in a ditch just by were strewed the bleached bones of Christian martyrs—sad memorials of dark days and darker deeds, now soon to be buried, though not forgotten, beneath a sanctuary which, while it enshrines the memory of many heroic sufferers, will honour the Saviour whom they loved, and for whom they died, and extend the knowledge of His

salvation. " The subdued, and yet eager manner," writes
Dr. Ryan, " in which the native Christians described what
had happened, was quite exciting to witness. It made old
stories of martyrdom appear quite recent and fresh. From
the parts interpreted and explained to me, I gathered the
following facts. That the Christians went to their death
with cheerful countenance, singing hymns as long as they
were able to do so. Straw was stuffed into their mouths
by their persecutors, to stop them, but until violently
hindered, they sang loudly the praises of God. Some of
the heathens, who were particularly desirous of seeing how
they behaved when the last hour of suffering came, confessed afterwards that nothing so impressed them as the
courageous demeanour and glad singing of those who
were being led to death. A large crowd seems to have
followed on the occasion to which our friends referred,
with shouting and imprecations against the Christians.
The victims were taken into the ditch, and made to bend
forward, and then two spears were struck into their bodies,
one on each side of the backbone, and when they fell
prostrate with their wounds, their heads were cut off, and
placed in rows along the edge of the ditch. The heads of
five members of one family were placed thus in a row on
one occasion, and thirteen others behind them, and were
left a long time there, till removed secretly, as I understood, by their friends. The whole scene," adds the
Bishop, " the description, the mournful tone of voice, the
affectionate earnestness of manner of those who told us,
some of whom had been for years exposed to the most
imminent danger themselves, all produced a most solemn
effect on the mind."

This, then, was the place to which Rasalama was conducted. But the scene did not disturb the deep calm of
her spirit. Though reviled by the heathen, she rested upon
the Saviour, and reviled not again. The only request
she made to her executioners was for a brief interval,
that she might pray. This was granted, and she kneeled
down upon the rocky ground. Some said, "Where is the
God she prays to, that He does not save her now?" Others
looked on with pity. But she was regardless of all around,
and held communion with her Divine Saviour; and while
thus commending her spirit into His hands, the executioners from behind buried their spears in her body. So
calm, so firm was this noble sufferer, that even the hard
men who took her life were constrained to say, "There is
some charm in the religion of the white people, which takes
away the fear of death;" while that courageous friend who
had accompanied her to the last, exclaimed, as he turned
from a spectacle at once so sorrowful and so sublime, "If
I might die so tranquil and happy a death, I would not be
unwilling to die for the Saviour too."

We cannot give a circumstantial history of the other
Christians who were apprehended with Rasalama. All of
them were condemned to hard bondage; but five of these
had the great comfort of working together. Their master,
indeed, Rainiharo, was their cruel persecutor, and they
had much to endure—toiling hard during the day, and
heavily ironed at night. But still they could speak often
one to another; and Paul, who, though weak in body was
strong in spirit, contributed not a little to the comfort of
his companions in tribulation by repeating the 46th Psalm,
and other passages of the Scriptures with which his memory

was stored. He possessed also a copy of the Psalter, and a Christian catechism, while another had preserved in secret a tract on the resurrection; and when all was dark and still, these precious treasures were drawn out from their hiding-places, and read aloud. This exercise and prayer lightened their heavy load, and brought them much peace.

Two others, David and Simeon, were assigned to a wretch, distinguished amongst his fellows for his cruel disposition—a bad pre-eminence, with which his treatment of these two Christians too well accorded. After three months, they were transferred to this tyrant's son, but not until they had drank the tangena, to show whether they possessed the power of witchcraft. This dangerous ordeal had nearly cost David's life, but God delivered him.

Amongst the nine who had been condemned, Rafaravary appears to have been the greatest sufferer. For five months she was kept in heavy chains, daily expecting to be led from prison to death. But her life was spared, and at the end of five months she was sold into perpetual slavery. Providentially, however, and without a suspicion of the kind on the part of her persecutors, her master was a humane man, and her mistress proved to be a relative. Some liberty was therefore allowed to her, and this she gladly improved; for as soon as her daily task was done, she hastened to the dwellings of her fellow-Christians. Amongst those with whom it was her delight to meet for prayer and praise, was Rafaralahy, the companion and comforter of Rasalama on her way to the scene of her martyrdom. He lived about two miles from the capital, and was making it the study of his life to minister to the wants and promote the welfare of his Christian brethren. He had compassion

on them in their bonds, and when in prison he visited
them. His property and his time were devoted to the
one great object of doing good. With this intent he had
built a house in a retired spot near his own dwelling, where
the brethren might meet for worship ; and here they were
often found in fellowship with each other and the Lord.
At the same time he laboured to draw others into the way
of life ; and amongst those for whose temporal and spiritual
interests he was peculiarly solicitous were three poor lepers.
These were outcasts from society, shunned and loathed by
all except this Christian man. But in him they found a
true friend. He sheltered them, fed them, and taught
them to read that blessed book which had brought peace
to his own spirit. And "with such sacrifices God was
well pleased." One of the lepers preceded his benefactor
to heaven, and there is reason to hope that the others have
followed him thither.

At length, a wretched man who owed Rafaralahy money
and much beside, hoping to release himself from his
obligation, accused his benefactor of being a Christian,
and of holding meetings in his own house. He was in
consequence seized, loaded with chains, and committed
to prison. But he "suffered as a Christian," and experienced that Divine support which enabled him, without
fear or faltering, to be "faithful unto death." During
the brief period of his confinement, severe measures were
employed to extort from him the names of his Christian
associates. But his unvarying answer to every persuasive,
and every threat, was, "Here am I, let the Queen do what
she pleases with me ; I have done it, but I will not accuse
my friends." After an imprisonment of two or three days,

the minister of death entered his prison, and when he inquired, " Which is Rafaralahy ?" the brave man promptly answered, " I am, sir !" His irons were then struck off, and he was led forth to the place of execution. Doubtless, as he walked towards it he remembered Rasalama, who had preceded him there, and probably did not forgot the strong sympathy and Christian love which then constrained him to draw near to her, and to whisper in her ear, " My sister, I will not leave you till the end." Though it does not appear that he sung, as she did, on his way to the fatal spot, we are told that he spoke to those around him of the Saviour, and of his joy in the near prospect of beholding Him. On reaching Ambohipotsy, following the example of Rasalama, he requested a brief space for prayer, and kneeling down upon the ground consecrated by her blood, and strewed with her unburied bones, he looked up steadfastly into heaven, prayed for his country and his brethren, and, having committed his soul to his Divine Redeemer, he arose from the ground, " ready to be offered." When the executioners were about to throw him down, he assured them that no force was necessary, as he was quite willing to die. He then laid himself upon the ground, and in a few moments he had entered into the joy of the Lord.

Immediately after his execution, the wife of Rafaralahy, and another female, were seized and subjected to torture to induce them to inculpate his associates. In a moment of weakness, produced by suffering and fear, they made the disclosure. Friends, however, were within hearing, who caught the names of some of the accused. Rafaravavy was one of them. Sitting with three of her fellow Christians, in conversation upon the subjects in which they were most deeply interested, a servant hastily entered the room and put a note into her hand. It conveyed the intelligence that Rafaralahy had been executed, and that, unless she and others instantly fled, they would also suffer. After a brief conference, the three women proceeded towards the city, and having reached the outskirts, they kneeled down, commended each other to God, and then separated, to meet no more on earth. Rafaravavy ventured to call at her master's house, though she expected to find officers awaiting her. After this, she went to confer with David, Simeon, and others of the accused, as to the course they should pursue. This appeared very clear to all of them. They therefore resolved upon immediate flight. As Simeon and David, who were slaves of Rainiharo, had money and cloth belonging to their master, their first concern was to draw up an accurate account of all sales and receipts, and to leave this paper for him, with what remained of his property. It was not surprising, when this evidence of integrity came into his hands, that the oppressor of the Christians was astonished, and exclaimed, " These would have made excellent servants, if they would but leave off their religion." It was now midnight, and time that the fugitives should leave the city. But this was not possible to Simeon, in consequence of the illness of his wife, nor to Paul and others, who lived too far off to be apprised of the movements of their brethren. Five only could avail themselves of the opportunity—Joseph, David and his wife, Andrianimanana, and Rafaravavy.

And it was well for them that they acted with promptitude, for, on the following morning, messengers with a death-warrant from the Queen hastened to every place where it was thought probable that Rafaravavy might be concealed.

A detailed history of these Christian fugitives has been already furnished in the deeply interesting narrative of Freeman and Johns. We shall, therefore, only briefly recall such of their many dangers and deliverances as most strikingly indicate the protecting care of Providence, and the strength of Christian principle, manifested not only by themselves, but by others. With this view we should remember that all who sheltered, fed, or in other ways assisted the Christians, exposed themselves to the same condemnation. But notwithstanding, wherever brethren dwelt, there was a home for the wandering; and thither they hasted, with a full assurance of a welcome and a hiding-place.

Fifty miles from the capital, at a place named Itanimanina, lived a Christian and his wife. To their abode the five fugitives first directed their steps. Here they met with the reception they expected; and, though exhausted with journeying and loss of sleep, the night after their arrival was mostly spent in prayer and praise, in the recital of recent events, and in the expression of anxiety for Paul, and others whom they had left behind. This anxiety, and the impossibility of concealing five strangers in one house, induced two of them to proceed to Paul's village, although the distance was thirty-five miles. But, on reaching their destination, they were distressed to learn that their friend was a prisoner. They therefore returned to Itanimanina.

About this time, a message came to them from another Christian in the same district, to this effect: "Let all the Christians who are compelled to run away for their lives come to me. I will take care of them. As long as I am

safe, they they are safe; and as long as I have food, they
shall share it." But just then this loving invitation was
not accepted, Joseph and David having previously arranged
to seek a refuge in the forest, far on the other side of the
capital. Thither, through dangers and with much difficulty,
they at length found their way, and here Simeon, who until
now had been concealed over an oven in a friend's house at
the capital, joined them. Only one man, and he was a servant of the Government, knew their hiding-place, and he
would not reveal it even to his nearest connections. As the
forest furnished fuel only, and not food, this noble specimen
of a friend and a brother, though naturally a timid man, ventured his own life to save theirs; and as often as he could
leave his home, he walked from fifty to sixty miles, with a
heavy burden of rice, over rugged roads and through the
tangled forest, to their hiding-place. Thus, by self-sacrific-
ing love and labour they were sustained nearly six months,
when it became necessary for them to seek another refuge.

Meanwhile, Rafaravavy remained at Itanimanina. But
soldiers were now upon her track, and caution was therefore
essential. Every morning, ere the day dawned, she crept
to a lonely mountain and hid herself amidst the craggy
rocks; at night she returned to her friend's house. But soon
even this care was no longer to avail her. Her place of
concealment had become known to Rainiharo, who at once
despatched soldiers to apprehend her. Knowing her daily
hiding-place, before they entered the village they searched
the mountain; but, as it rained, contrary to her custom, Rafaravavy had that day remained within. Having failed to
find her amidst the rocks, the soldiers hastened towards the
house unperceived, had come within sight of it, and were

hastening towards the door. There was now but a step between her and death; but, by one of those simple, and, as some would suppose, insignificant agencies which Divine Providence often employs, the Christian woman was rescued from her imminent danger. Though the soldiers created no alarm within the house, their hasty movements frightened some crows that were near it; and as Sarah, Rafaravavy's companion, inferred from their noise that the birds were stealing some rice which had been spread out to dry, she ran out to drive the depredators away, when, to her surprise and alarm, she saw the two soldiers. In a low tone she warned her friend of the danger, who had just time enough to creep under a bedstead in the next room, and to cover herself up with a mat, ere the men entered. Happily, they did not search the house, but for an hour Rafaravavy heard all they had to say respecting her, and the orders which had been issued for her death. But, calm in the midst of this peril, she comforted herself with the words, " Be not afraid of sudden fear, neither of the desolation of the wicked when it cometh, for the Lord shall be thy confidence, and shall keep thy foot from being taken." Often, in other days of danger, did she and her friends recall this remarkable deliverance, and strengthen themselves in the Lord.

But it was now quite time for Rafaravavy and Sarah—together with their kind and most disinterested protectors, who had cheerfully risked all, and were willing to lay down their own necks for the sake of their brethren—to seek a safer habitation. After hiding for a short time in the houses of friendly neighbours, they travelled all night to a distant village, where they knew they would find Christian

A VILLAGE IN MADAGASCAR.

hospitality. Having been concealed here for a few days, they travelled some distance to the abode of a relative, but had scarcely reached it, when they heard that soldiers were searching the neighbourhood for some woman that had run away. They therefore returned to the place they had left the day before, but the first intelligence that greeted them was that a party of soldiers was then in the village in quest of them. The pious woman who warned them of the danger hid them for that night in a pit, from which dreary refuge she conducted them on the following morning to a plantation of her own. Here, for some days, they were un-discovered, though they saw the men who were searching for them pass their hiding-place.

There were now about a hundred soldiers prosecuting the search. It was therefore arranged that they should be-come two bands; still, many were the "hair-breadth 'scapes" of both parties. Once, as Rafaravavy with her two com-panions reached the crest of a hill, a company of soldiers was seen marching towards them; and as she could not run like the others, it was only by lying half buried in a bog, surrounded by rushes, that she eluded observation.

But the hearts and hopes of the wanderers were now set upon the house of another Christian friend, where they knew that a loving welcome awaited them. Under the shadow of night, and through a country infested with robbers, they pressed on towards the much longed-for rest-ing place. At length, wearied with the journey, they reached their destination. As soon as their friend saw them, he burst into tears; but they were tears of joy at their unhoped-for deliverance out of the power of the armed bands who were scouring that part of the country in search of them. Here, again, was another striking manifestation of Christian confidence and affection, which it is refreshing to contemplate. The fugitives, though fully aware of the danger to which their presence under his roof would expose their friend, nevertheless went thither assured that his love to them for Christ's sake was superior to danger and stronger than death; whilst he, deaf to the suggestions of expediency, and to the pleadings of selfishness, was ready to risk all for the privilege of affording these persecuted friends all the aid and comfort which his loving heart could prompt, or his liberal hand supply.

It was, however, not an easy thing to shield these stranger guests from observation. At first an attempt was made to dig a hiding-place for them under a part of the house; but, failing in this, their host fixed a tent in the centre of a plantation of which he was the proprietor, where the high grass, and a prohibition against trespassers, promised well for their safety. Here, for three months, they were supplied and guarded. But these were not months of mere solitary musings and silent devotions. In common with their friend, the Christians desired to spend it for the profit of others as well as themselves; and this desire was fulfilled. Every Sabbath a band of brethren met together for worship. And some who were not be-lievers were nevertheless intrusted with the strangers' secret, and admitted to their society. Thus nearly twenty, during their sojourn, learned to read, and several members of the good man's family became decided followers of the Saviour. How obviously in this instance did the kind-ness shown in the name of a disciple, meet with its rich reward!

At length the soldiers, foiled in their search, returned
to the capital, and the Christians felt as if they could once
more breathe freely. Just about this time, a letter from a
friend informed them that Mr. Johns had come to Tamatave to aid their escape. But they were now on the
western side of Tananarivo, a long distance from the coast,
which could only be reached by passing through the capital.
Yet, though the danger of the journey was imminent, their
desire of deliverance, and their trust in Him who had
hitherto been their shield, decided them to make the
attempt.

Notwithstanding her disguise, as she was entering the
capital, Rafaravavy was recognised by a slave, who reported
the discovery to her former master. Happily, he disregarded the girl's assertion, and took no measures to ascertain its truth. While in the capital, the house where she
was hiding herself was searched by a party of men, and
once more she experienced a marvellous escape.

All the fugitives were now in Antananarivo, and here
they remained while two friends hastened down to Tamatave to make arrangements with Mr. Johns for their escape.
On their return the party commenced their perilous journey
towards the coast. For four days and nights after their
departure they did not enter a house, and their fears kept
them in a state of almost sleepless vigilance. But God's
word, and passages from the " Pilgrim's Progress,"
which shadowed forth something of their own condition,
brought them peace in the midst of trouble. As they had
to pass though villages where Rafaravavy was known, and
to shun the observation of many soldiers who were travelling the same road the constant and severe strain upon

their spirits and strength was most exhausting. Once and again they lost their way in the almost pathless forest, but they pressed on until they reached the river Mangoro, which swarms with crocodiles, and the only way to cross which was in a Government canoe. Happily, the boatman had no suspicions, and made no inquiry. At length, through difficulties and dangers which cannot here be detailed, their weary eyes were gladdened by the gleam of the sea breaking upon the coast. But now their food was exhausted, and the distance to Tamatave was still great. There, however, a kind and influential Christian friend was expecting them, and as soon as he heard of their approach, he sent a canoe to convey them to a house which he had prepared for them in a situation where the danger of discovery was but slight. Who can describe the gratitude and joy with which, on entering this new abode, they united with their protector in reading the 16th chapter of the Gospel by John, and in pouring out the fulness of their hearts before God in prayer and praise!

After a few days, disguised as sailors they embarked for the Mauritius. How they were received at that island, at the Cape of Good Hope, and in England, need not here be told. Thankful and joyful as they were, however, in view of their own great deliverance, their hearts turned sorrowfully back towards Madagascar, as they thought of the dear friends they had left behind them there, and received the intelligence that an order had been issued by the Queen, that, wherever Christians were discovered, they should be tied by their hands and feet, that a pit should be dug upon the spot, and that, having been thrust into it head foremost, boiling water should be poured upon their bodies until they were dead. This was rendered more bitter by a letter from their fugitive brethren, in which they write, " We have heard of the orders of the Queen respecting us, and in what manner we are to be put to death. We still confide in the compassion of the Saviour ; but we ask, ' Can you do anything to rescue us ?' We think of the death awaiting us. The spirit is willing, but the flesh is weak."

Foiled in all her efforts to apprehend the Christians, and learning that Rafaravavy and others, for whom the soldiers had long and wearily searched, had effected their escape, the fury of the Queen flamed forth more fiercely than before. It was enough now if any were merely suspected of being Christians, to bring them under the oppressor's rod. Three women dwelt in the capital, who were supposed to be Christians. Two of these were the wives of Simeon and David, then safe in a Christian land. Without positive evidence of their Christianity, an official was ordered to apprehend them. Happily, when he reached the house where he expected to find them, one was absent, and another had fled on hearing his errand ; but the rough man rudely seized the third woman, and while beating her, a copy of the Bible fell from her dress. This, of course, made her guilt manifest. She was in consequence cruelly scourged, even to fainting, with a view to extort from her the names of her companions. But torture could not loose her tongue, or shake her constancy. She was therefore condemned to perpetual slavery, while her friends sought a refuge in the forest.

But all could not flee. One of these was a young woman whose eminent piety, while it secured for her the warm love of her Christian associates, called forth the bitter hatred of

her own family, all of whom were bigoted heathens. Her
father's house was closed against her; she was scorned and
repudiated by her husband, while all her other relatives
sympathized with their anger and aversion. Having obtained her condemnation as a Christian, she was sentenced
to unredeemable slavery. It might have been imagined
that a doom so severe would have satisfied them; but it
was not so. They thirsted and plotted for her life, and
at last, by a subtle device, obtained a decree which compelled her to take the tangena. The poison-cup proved fatal.
The wretched relatives had now satiated their vengeance,
but they had added another to the honoured band of
Madagascar martyrs. The name of this Christian sufferer
was Ravahiny, and it will be remembered with love and
honour, when that of her deluded murderers will have
perished.

In the hope of rendering valuable aid to the Christian
sufferers, in July, 1840, Mr. Johns, who had remained
until this time at Mauritius, ventured to revisit the capital;
but on reaching it, he received the sad intelligence that
fourteen Christians had been captured, and were then in
chains, awaiting their trial. Their history was soon learned.
Two years before, like so many of their brethren, a party
of sixteen resolved, if possible, to flee from the tyranny of
the Queen. With this view they set out towards Tamatave, and had, after long wandering, reached a village
called Beforona, which was within three or four days'
journey of the coast, when the suspicion of some officers
who saw them there was awakened by their appearance,
and by the circumstance that they travelled through bye-
paths, and at night. They were, in consequence, taken into

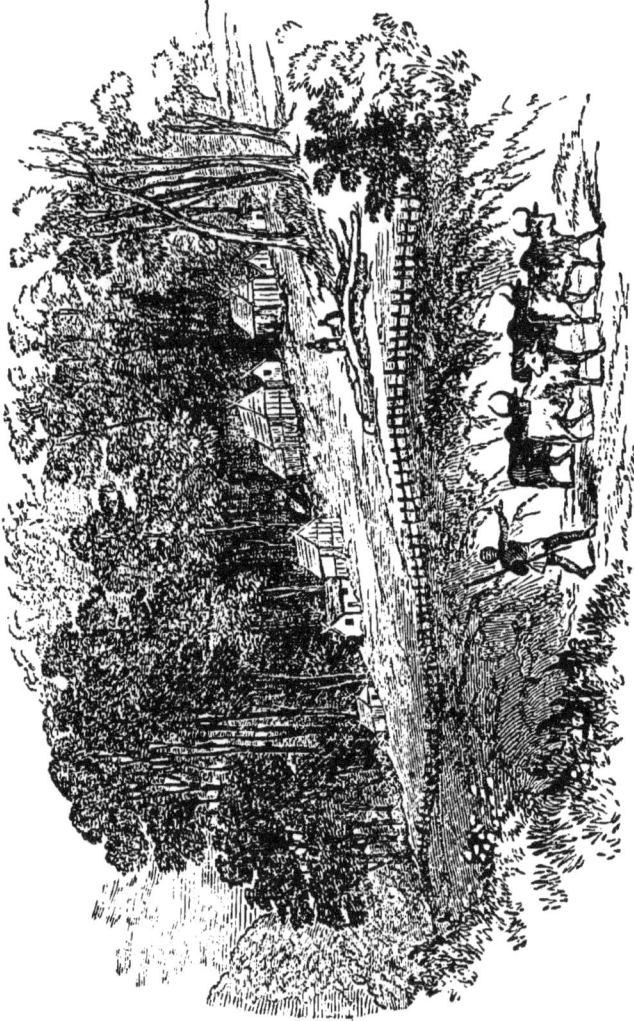

A VILLAGE IN MADAGASCAR.

custody. After three days' examination, during which
nothing of importance had been elicited, they resolved to
say who they were. Accordingly, one of them stood forth
and thus spoke : " Since you ask us again and again, we
will tell you. We are not robbers, nor murderers, we
are praying people ; and if this make us guilty in the kingdom of the Queen, then, whatsoever she does, that we
must submit to suffer." " Is this, then," inquired the
officer, "your final answer, whether for life or for death ?"
" It is," they rejoined, " our final answer, whether for life
or for death."

The captives were then bound, and marched off towards
Antananarivo. Two of them, however, happily escaped
during the night, but the remainder were brought to the
capital. Though they well knew what awaited them, their
faith triumphed over fear. Firm and calm throughout the
examination to which they were separately subjected, they
witnessed a good confession, and avowed their readiness
to die for the name of the Lord Jesus.

This sad intelligence greatly distressed Mr. Johns, and
the more so because he knew that no appeals to the justice
or the mercy of the inexorable Queen would turn her from
her purpose. His only refuge, and that of the Christians
with whom he communed in secret, was the Divine throne.
And there they often met, and the burden of their prayers
was that their brethren might not faint in the day of
danger, or prove faithless in the prospect of death. And
in this God gave them the desire of their hearts.

Early one morning, after he had been in the capital
but a few days, Mr. Johns was startled by the firing of
cannon. This was an unusual sound, and he well knew

that it betokened something extraordinary; but what, he
could not learn. At length the heavy tidings reached
him, and oppressed his heart, that nine of the fourteen Christians were that day to die. He knew them
all, and loved them much. They had been amongst the
first ripe fruit of missionary labour, and were deservedly
honoured by their brethren. Amongst them was Paul and
Joshua, with their wives, and the wife of David, who had
escaped to England. But besides these, there was another
who was greatly beloved, and whose name and memory
are still fragrant in Madagascar. This was Ramanisa, who
took the baptismal name of Josiah. Before the persecution, he had been a faithful preacher of the Gospel; and
when trouble came, he was not only himself prepared to
endure it, but was earnest and active in strengthening
others. Despairing of the Christians' liberty, for which he
longed, he resolved to accompany the fifteen in their
attempt to find a refuge and a resting-place beyond their
native shores. And greatly did they value his presence.
He was to them a guide and a pastor, ministering counsel
and consolation where they were most needed, while they
were lurking in caves, and travelling by night, and wandering in forest solitudes. In these dark days his cheering
words and fervent prayers made them "strong in the
Lord," and "joyful in tribulation." This good man was
the author of a hymn much prized, and often sung by
the persecuted Christians when scattered by the storm, or
fleeing from their foes, or hiding in secret places far off
from the friends and the homes they loved. It is now in
the Malagasy hymn book, and from the sacred associations
which cluster around it, it will long retain its power over

the hearts of Christians in that land. The following is a translation.

> " Loud to the Lord your voices raise,
> Extol His name, exalt His praise,
> Publish the wonders of His hand
> O'er all the earth, in every land.
>
> Tell of the pity of the Lord,
> Of grace and mercy :—preach the Word,
> For wonderful to us appears
> That love for us He ever bears.
>
> Though guilty, we're with pardon crown'd ;
> Condemn'd and lost, we now are found ;
> Though dead, new life to us is given,
> And everlasting life in heaven.
>
> Oh! God, our God, to Thee we cry,
> Jesus, the Saviour, be Thou nigh ;
> Oh! sacred Spirit, hear our prayer,
> And save the afflicted from despair.
>
> Scarce can we find a place for rest,
> Save dens and caves, with hunger press'd ;
> Yet Thy compassion is our bliss,
> Pilgrims amidst a wilderness."

The day of the martyrdom of these true-hearted sufferers was a peculiarly sorrowful one to the solitary Missionary then at Antananarivo, and to their Christian survivors. Throughout the morning, his heart sunk as the heavy booming of the cannon fell upon his ear, and as he watched the lines of soldiers marching towards the dreaded Ambohipotsy. At noon, officers commissioned by the Queen made the public announcement that nine praying people had been condemned, and would die that day ; but it was not until nearly four o'clock that they were led forth from prison. They were then stripped, and each of them was slung up to a pole by their hands and feet, which had been firmly tied together. In this most painful position, they were borne upon the shoulders of four men to the place of execution. Calm and strong, they endured the torture without murmuring, and when the fatal spot was reached, they showed that death had no sting for them. Like Rasalama and Rafaralahy, they were sentenced to be speared, and the appointed signal for the execution was the firing of a cannon. All were now awaiting the fatal moment. The match was applied, but the cannon burst, and the gunner was much injured, which accident the people deemed a bad omen. But the Queen's command admitted of no delay, and as the echoes of the bursting gun were dying away amongst the distant hills, these nine faithful witnesses for Christ were rising to join the noble army of the martyrs, and to take their places in that world where "they hear not the voice of the oppressor."

There were still very many, not less than two hundred, "destitute, afflicted, tormented," who "wandered in deserts and in mountains, and in dens and caves of the earth," and whose condition called forth the strong sympathy and solicitude of many British Christians. Intensely anxious for the escape of their persecuted brethren, the Directors of the London Missionary Society instructed their devoted Missionary, Mr. Johns, who continued at the Mauritius, principally with this object in view, to spare neither labour nor expense for its attainment. And in that admirable man they possessed an agent in whose judgment, energy, and self-denial they could fully confide. But although he and other friends of the oppressed employed every effort they could devise, the coast was now so closely watched and guarded by the Queen's emissaries, that escape for a single Christian seemed all but hopeless. This was the more distressing from the fact that their sufferings and dangers were continually increasing. Many of the Christians had been hunted by the Queen's officers, with the instinct and ferocity of bloodhounds, until they had been driven into wild and almost inaccessible heights of the mountains, where there was little shelter and less food. Two of these wanderers risked their lives in order to visit a Christian friend at Tamatave, in the hope that some method might be devised for the rescue of their brethren. But with heavy hearts they were compelled to carry back the sad tidings that little or nothing could be done. Wonderful, indeed, was the power of principle, and the energy of Divine grace, which, in circumstances so appalling, made these Christians strong to suffer, and enabled them in the endurance of trial, and in the face of death, to "quit themselves like men."

While the two hundred scattered over the country were fleeing from their persecutors, many Christians still remained in and around the capital: but most of these were either prisoners or slaves. The year after Mr. Johns' visit, some of them thus wrote to a friend at Tamatave:—

"Our salutations to you, say the little flock in Madagascar. Through the blessing of God on us, we are yet alive, and do not forget you and all our friends. This is what we have to say to you, beloved Father! The affliction which has occurred to us, and of which you have heard, greatly increases. Executions, ordeals, and

miseries increase throughout the country. * * The
wretchedness of the people is unutterable. * * Do rescue
us, beloved Father! if possible. If God be not our defence,
we are dead men. We are as a city set on a hill, that
cannot be hid.

" Our Government service continues to be very severe.
When the children of Israel served under Pharaoh, perhaps
they obtained some little respite, at any rate, by night;
but *ours* is incessant labour! We must work both night
and day."

In another letter to the same friend, they say—" You
exhort us to take courage, and not to be cast down. We
accept your exhortation, and we all take confidence and
rejoice. And you further ask us if there is any thing you
want, adding that we should write and tell you. Now,
there is one point on which we are much afflicted—our
want of Bibles. We can conceal them, though there are
many enemies. Those we have are quite worn out.

" And with regard to the means of our support, it may
be said we have, and have not. All our property was
taken from us. However, this is the word of the Lord—
' Consider the ravens; they sow not, they reap not, yet
God feedeth them.' And just so, dear friend, the Lord
has pity on us."

During the next year (1842), the cruelty of the Queen
and the constancy of the Christians continued. Five more
were at this time added to the honoured roll of Madagascar
martyrs. Two of these were on their way back from a place
where they had gone to seek a refuge for themselves and their
brethren, where they could also instruct the inhabitants.
They belonged to Vonizongo, where the prisoners were taken.

Their names were Ratsitahina and Rabearahaba. Like many who had suffered before them, they were put to the torture, to extort from them the names of their brethren, but the attempt was in vain; all they would acknowledge was that they had themselves prayed, and followed the practices of the praying people. Just before they suffered, a messenger from their Christian friends found his way to them, to whom they whispered—"Let them not fear that we shall disclose their names. We shall do them no harm; but say farewell! If we do not meet again here on earth, we shall meet in the future life." They were executed in the market-place of Vonizongo, and their heads were then stuck upon poles, to warn others not to follow their example.

In a very affecting letter, written about this time, one of the Christians says—"Our trials are greater than ever, and the number of the persecuted is increasing daily. The officers of the Queen are searching for them everywhere, to put them to death. We do not know what to do, as the road in all directions is almost impassable, and our hiding-places are nearly all known to our enemies."

"The present trials of the Christians," writes another, "are very heavy to *flesh and blood*, but they are even light to be borne by the mind and soul that lean upon the Lord. * * I told you, in a former letter, that the Queen ordered the tangena to be given to me, but, by the blessing of God, I got over it. Join me, O my beloved friend! in praising the Lord, who hath blessed and preserved me alive. Five of our friends are hiding themselves with me, and I shall take particular care of them; but others go from place to place to seek for something to support nature."

In October of this year, three more laid down their lives

rather than deny the Saviour. Some unknown person had
affixed a paper to a wall in Antananarivo, with something
written upon it which displeased the Queen. The writer
was commanded to give himself up in four days. Raharo,
who had been one of the twelve principal teachers in the
reign of Radama, was, with other Christians, apprehended
upon suspicion. They were forced to drink the tangena,
which proved fatal to Raharo. But as another Christian,
called Ratsimilay, was detected in an attempt to save his
friend from the effects of the poison cup, he was condemned
to die; whilst a third, Imamonjy, was sentenced with him
to be cut into small pieces, and then burnt.

Thus far we have sketched the history of eight years of
the persecution in Madagascar. Within this short period,
hundreds of Christians had been condemned to chains or
slavery, while others were hiding in the forests and the
mountains, and at least seventeen had suffered death.
And for what had they endured such things?   For their
religion. This was their only crime—their enemies themselves being judges.   And had they denied the faith, their
property, liberty, and lives would have been safe. A word
would have sufficed for this purpose. But no! They took
joyfully the spoiling of their goods; they cheerfully endured
bonds and imprisonment, and counted not even their lives
dear unto themselves, so that they might win Christ, and
be found in Him.   Such noble virtues, under almost any
circumstances, would constrain the thoughtful observer
to exclaim—"This is the finger of God!"   But this
acknowledgment will be made with double emphasis when
we consider the history of these heroic sufferers. Had
they been nurtured in the midst of Christian associations,

with the superior advantages of mental and spiritual training, and trained in the ways of God from their youth, the manifestation of piety like theirs—in circumstances the most trying, and in such forms as have invested with the brightest lustre the most honoured names recorded in the martyrology of the Church—would have compelled us to "glorify God in them." But that such nobleness of character, that such triumphs of principle, that such superiority to every sordid and selfish motive, that such faith in God and fidelity to conscience, that such unyielding constancy and unfaltering fearlessness should have been matured and developed in those who from their early days had been surrounded by the dark and debasing influences of paganism, is a phenomenon to baffle philosophers and moralists, and one which only admits of a Christian solution.

And if any thing more were necessary to prove that God was certainly with them, we might find it in the remarkable fact that, even now, when in the view of sense there was so much to deter others from treading the same path of sorrow and danger, these sufferers could write, "The number of learners is greatly increasing," and that several of the people had lately joined them.

Although the Queen's command, enforced by fearful threats, that all books should be delivered up had been urgent, many of the Christians, both in the capital and in the country, had disobeyed it, and had hid—often buried— their Bibles in the earth. But the copies thus preserved were few, and many of them had been so diligently read by their possessors, or so often lent to less fortunate friends, that they were almost worn out. What, therefore, they desired above every earthly good, was a supply of this sacred treasure. "Exceedingly afflicted are we," they write, "on account of the fewness of the Bibles here with us, and we exceedingly desire to have more. We are thirsting for them, for the Bible is our companion and friend, to instruct, and search in, thoroughly, when in secrecy and silence, and to comfort us in our grief and tribulation. Send us *many*, for even then they will not be enough, and let them be small in print, so as to be easily hidden." In the same letter they add—"As to the condition of the country, it is still dark, and there is still persecution by the Queen. Nevertheless, the people are going forward. Blessed be God! who thus prospers them." They further state, that every Saturday the men travel a long way to some hill or valley, "so as to get beyond the reach of the people, that none may see, that they may spend the Sabbath together in worshipping God. But the women were not strong enough to walk so far; and this," says the writers of the letter "makes us feel very much on account of the sorrow of those who cannot go."

Thus the Christians of Madagascar, though "faint," were "yet pursuing" the pathway of faith and holiness. But still they were often "cast down," though "not destroyed." This was especially the case with those in the capital. From the year 1840, that dreadful time when so many had perished, they had been so closely watched, that it became increasingly difficult to escape discovery. Since that day, five weary years had rolled along, and still no change had come. God was indeed with them, and His Word was their light in this great darkness. But they were prone to cry, "Why standest thou afar off, O God! Why hidest thou thyself in time of trouble?" And they needed the exhortation, "Consider Him, who endured such contradiction of sinners against Himself, lest ye be weary and faint in your minds."

But a great revival was now at hand. Suddenly, a bright light broke through the black cloud which had so long hung over the faithful sufferers. At that time there was a youth residing at the capital, named Rainaka. He had become a Christian, and, subsequent to the commencement of the persecution, a preacher of the Gospel; and very bold and very earnest was he in the service of the Saviour. Regardless of royal decrees and legal penalties, he laboured with heart and soul to draw others to the cross. Encouraged by his bright and bold example, the Christians assembled in a large house for worship three times a week. It was a daring venture, but God honoured it. Many strangers were drawn to listen to the young Apostle, and not a few of them believed the Gospel. Thus, in a short time about a hundred were added to the proscribed Christians. But this was not all. Amongst these new adherents, there was one of the very last men in Madagascar whom they expected to find there. This was Rakoto-radama, (which means *son* of Radama), the Queen's only child, then about seventeen years of age.

In what way the preaching of the zealous Rainaka influenced the young Prince, we do not know; but the good fruits in his character and conduct soon showed themselves, and have continued to this day. Five months after he had joined the Christians, twenty-one of them were seized by the Queen's order; and as she was incensed at their boldness and augmented numbers, there is every reason to believe that she had resolved to destroy them all. But now, for the

first time, young Rakoto placed himself between his heathen
mother and his Christian brethren.   He went to her and
begged for their lives.   As she loved her son, his earnest
entreaties somewhat softened her hard heart, and saved the
Christians from death ; but nine were compelled to drink
the tangena, one of whom died, and the rest were sold as
slaves, or held in chains.   At length, however, by the exer-
tions of the Prince, they all regained their liberty, but not
until those who were in prison had been made the instruments of the conversion of their gaolers.   How greatly the
Christians were encouraged by these wonderful proofs of
God's presence and favour, will appear from a letter written
by some of them in February 1846, to the Missionaries
at Mauritius.

"We went up to Antananarivo, and there met (in a religious assembly) with the Queen's son, and the persecuted
Christians, nothing disheartened by the temptations of Satan,
though they may suffer in bonds: and those Christians
who are not persecuted, we found increasing exceedingly;
yea, becoming indeed many.   And Rakoto, the Queen's
son, makes very great progress in the love of the Lord, by
God's blessing, and is able to assemble some Christians
with himself every night to thank and praise God.   Oh!
blessed be God, who has caused His mercy to descend
upon Rakoto and all the people!"

From the time when first convinced that the Scriptures
were of God, the Prince has continued the fast friend
of the Christians, and how valuable that friendship has
proved during the dark and stormy years that followed,
we shall see.   He was cautious, indeed, but he practised
no concealment, even from his mother.   She and others

knew perfectly what he was and what he did. He could not indeed openly defy the law; but, wrote the Christians, " He comes regularly with us in the woods on Sundays to pray and sing, and read the Bible; and he often takes some of us home with him to explain to him the Word of Truth, and he keeps his mother from doing us any harm." But he was accomplishing even more than this just then. The printing-press had been long stopped, and was now out of repair. But the Prince used means to get it again into working order, that it might print the Bible, and religious books. This was a very bold proceeding upon his part, and strikingly shows how firm and fearless he was, even though so young. By the great favour of God, the good promise then given has since, and is now, largely fulfilled.

The agency through which the Prince was first brought into association with the Christians, and subsequently to their secret meetings, appears to have been a Christian young man, whose uncle frequented the palace on business, and who was occasionally admitted with him. Influenced, as all the Christians obviously were, by a fervent desire to diffuse the Gospel, this young man contrived to bring the subject under the notice of Rakoto. Thus the interest in Christianity which, happily for that great country, has suffered no decline, was originally awakened in the Prince's mind. Subsequently, the same young disciple drew him to the assemblies of the Christians, where, as already stated, he heard the Gospel from the fervid lips of Rainaka.

" From this time," writes one of them, " he was very diligent in conversing with us on the subject of

E

Christianity ; and at length he invited some of us into his house in the palace-yard, to converse with him in secret, and we were thus frequently invited to his house to converse with him."

It may be well supposed that such a change in Rakoto filled the enemies of Christianity with burning anger, and that many would have rejoiced had he been numbered with the martyrs. Amongst those who felt thus was the chief minister of the Queen. Long had he been the unrelenting foe of the Christians, and well knowing how much they were protected and encouraged by the Prince, he thirsted for the young man's life, and only waited for a favourable moment to assail it. So one day when he was with the Queen, and had, as he imagined, a suitable opportunity for indulging his wicked desire, he said to her, "Your son, Madam, is a Christian ; he prays with the Christians, and encourages them in this new doctrine. We are lost if your Majesty does not stop the Prince in this strange way." "But," replied the Queen, "he is my son, my only, my beloved son ! Let him do what he pleases; if he wishes to become a Christian, let him : he is my beloved son !" Thus, happily the love of the mother proved stronger than the hatred of the persecutor.

But natural affection was strong even in Rainiharo himself. This appeared soon afterwards. He had a favourite nephew who had become a Christian, and had attended the secret meetings of the proscribed and hated sect. Without the slightest suspicion of the truth, one day Rainiharo sent this nephew as a spy to one of their well-known resorts, with a strict injunction to take the names of all who were there. To this the nephew made no objection ; but in-

stantly hastened to the place where prayer was wont to
be made, told the brethren why he had come and who had
sent him, and then asked them to separate, lest they should
be se n by their foes.   On his return home, Rainiharo inquired for the list.   "There is none," replied the youth.
"Young man!" he sternly exclaimed, "you have disobeyed
my oiders.   Why have you done this?   Your head must
fall, for you show that you also are a Christian."   With
simplicity and godly sincerity the nephew said, "Yes, my
uncle, I *am* a Christian; and, if you please, you may put
me to death, for I pray."   The persecutor was confounded
at the answer.   For a moment he was silent, and gazed
with wonder at the youth, who, firm and calm, stood prepared to meet the consequences of his bold confession;
but the only reply the persecutor could make was, "Oh
no; you shall not die."

But the son of the sovereign, and her chief councillor,
were not the only persons of high rank who at that period
avowed their attachment to the new religion.   Rakoto had
a cousin named Ramonja.   He was a son of the Queen's
sister, and a great favourite of the Queen herself; and it is
not improbable that her partiality to him arose, in part at
least, from the devotion with which he supported the
superstitious customs of the country, and the bitter hostility which, in common with his aunt, he cherished against
the Christians; for at this time he was one of their most
devermined persecutors.

But as there was a close intimacy between him and
the Prince, it was not long ere their conversation turned
upon the subject so interesting to both of them, though in
so different a way.   The result was, that through the efforts

of Rakoto, his cousin abandoned the idols and embraced the Gospel, and from that time became the friend and protector of the Christians, and one of the most devout and consistent of their number.

But these conversions were not the only circumstances which at this time cheered the hearts of the Christians. At no previous period had the desire to learn to read been more manifest. But as the teachers subjected themselves to heavy pains and penalties, they very prudently refused to instruct any but those whose character and conduct warranted the belief that they were influenced by love to the Word of God. Yet, notwithstanding this restriction, they tell us that not less than a hundred and fifty of their number were engaged in this work, all of whom were constantly surrounded by pupils, to the number of from six to upwards of twenty.

But there were, at the same time, more decisive proofs of the Divine favour even than this. Early in the year 1847, one of the Christians thus describes their spiritual condition. "How wonderful is the power of God as we see it now in the spirit of anxious inquiry produced in the minds of the people! They come to seek the Lord in the prison with the prisoners, in the hiding-places of the persecuted, in the mountains and in the dingles. Whenever and wherever they can meet with any calling upon the name of the Lord, thither they resort. Sweet are the cords of imprisonment to the prisoners—they are not ashamed of them any longer."

Another writer relates an incident which was not without its influence upon many of the weak and wavering. A heathen man, hoping to bring back the Prince to heathenism, went to him with the grave assurance, that if an attempt were made to set fire to the house of the idol Ramahavaly it could not be burned.   The Prince resolved that the experiment should be tried, and first, he ordered the keeper of the idol to make the attempt.   As, however, he merely threw a piece of lighted cow-dung upon the roof, which immediately rolled off, it failed.   Two Christians then volunteered for the service, and the work was soon done, the Prince all the while watching the blazing temple from the balcony of his house, and manifesting his delight at its destruction.

Thus, by various indications of His presence and grace, God was preparing His servants for persecution more terrible than any which they had hitherto endured.   And amongst the exciting causes to which that persecution must be traced, are those which had brought the greatest gladness to their hearts—the signs of progress and prosperity.   These, so cheering to themselves, were hateful to their foes.   The increasing numbers and boldness of the Christians; the openness with which they assembled, and read, and prayed in defiance of law; and still more, the fact that her son, her nephew, and others of high rank had embraced their opinions, filled the Queen and her abettors with rage almost amounting to madness.   It is at this period that Rambosalama, the brother of Ramonga, first comes prominently into view.   Adopted by the Queen as her successor to the throne, prior to the birth of her son, this young man had always regarded Rakoto as his enemy and supplanter. He had long been opposed to the new religion; but the Prince's adhesion to it increased his hostility, and made him, there is reason to believe, a chief instigator of the per-

secution of 1849, as well as an active agent in the discovery and impeachment of Christians. He sent spies in
all directions, and employed other means which proved but
too effectual in bringing suffering upon the objects of his
aversion.

The earliest indication of the coming tempest appeared
on the 19th of February, 1849, in an order from the
Queen to destroy two houses which had been used for
Christian worship. Prince Ramonja interposed with a
claim upon one of them, but it was disallowed, and the
buildings were razed to the ground. During the next two
days, nine Christians were consigned to prison. One of
these had been an officer of the army, and after the loss of
his sight, had become a faithful preacher of the Gospel.

In the course of the following week the people were twice
called together to a kabary; and when they were assembled,
an officer thus addressed them : " 'I ask you,' saith the
Queen, ' what is the reason you will not forsake the very
root of this new religion and mode of worship? For I
have deprived officers of their honour, put some to death,
reduced others to unredeemable slavery, and you still per-
severe in practising this new religion. What is the reason
why you will not renounce it?' " Bold must those have
been who could answer these words of the Queen. But
such there were amongst the Christians, two of whom thus
replied in the name of their companions : "We are restrained by reverence for God and His law !" It was a
noble reply, and was influenced by the same spirit which
constrained the apostolic appeal, " Whether it be right in
the sight of God to hearken unto you more than unto God,
judge ye."

But all the recorded confessions made by the Christians at this time breathe the same spirit. " When," said one, "the Queen inquires why we have not abandoned this worship, we reply that there is a law in this worship, which makes us afraid of God if we steal, or if we commit murder, or if we deceive our fellows, or if we do any evil. *Therefore we have not forsaken it.*" " We make supplication," said another, " to God for the Queen, for her subjects, for our wives and children, and for all the good we need, and as we can do this, we have not forsaken the religion."

Nine Christians who had refused to take the prescribed oath were wrapped in mats and loaded with chains; to this number an officer of the army and a soldier were added shortly afterwards. On being again urged to submit to the Queen, they unitedly refused, and added, " It is God that we worship, for He, and He only, can do all things for us, and we will pray to none but Him."

Immediately after this, five others were accused, two of them attendants upon Prince Ramonja. One man, named Ramany, stood up before the multitude, and with a courage and calmness like that of the martyr Stephen, said, " I believe in God, for He alone can do all things for me; but as for swearing by the Queen, or by one's mother or sister, or father or brother, a lie is a lie still, whether you swear to it or not. I believe in God, and put my trust in Jesus Christ, the Saviour and Redeemer of all that believe in Him." He and his companions were then put in chains, and cast into prison.

The following account of the examination of some of these witnesses for Christ was given to Mr. Ellis.

"Do you pray to the sun, or the moon, or the earth?" asked the officer.

"I do not pray to these," was the answer, "for the hand of God made them."

Officer. "Do you pray to the twelve sacred mountains?"

Christian. "I do not pray to them, for they are mountains."

O. "Do you pray to the idols that render sacred the Kings?"

C. "I do not pray to them, for the hand of man made them."

O. "Do you pray to the ancestors of the sovereigns?"

C. "Kings and rulers are given by God, that we should serve and obey them, and render them homage. Nevertheless, they are only men like ourselves. When we pray, we pray to God alone."

O. "You make distinct, and observe the Sabbath day?"

C. "That is the day of the great God; for in six days, the Lord made all His works. But God rested on the seventh, and He caused it to be holy; and I rest, to keep sacred that day."

There are some things in these confessions which deserve special notice. Had there been at that most exciting time, and amongst a people so recently brought out of heathen darkness into light so marvellous as that of the Gospel, some indications of ill-regulated zeal, an undue desire for a martyr's crown, or a low estimate of life and of death, we might not have been surprised. But never have sufferers evinced less of irrational enthusiasm. Though they employed every justifiable precaution to evade the penalties, they resorted to no unworthy arts of concealment or compromise. And in all their answers to the royal requirements, we clearly discover that the will of Christ was their only law. Each could truly say, "But so did not I because of the fear of God." Hence the simplicity and strength with which they gave the reasons of their refusal. Nor should those reasons themselves be unnoticed. Independently of other sources of information, they make it evident that the only crime alleged against them was their Christianity. Their worst foes could "find no occasion against them except concerning the law of their God." Upon this point the testimony of their oppressors is the most explicit. In all the Queen's edicts their evil practices are minutely described. The following is a specimen of many similar documents.

"These are the things which shall not be done, saith the Queen. The saying to others, Believe and obey the Gospel; the practice of baptism; the keeping of the Sabbath as a day of rest; the refusing to swear by one's father, or mother, or sister, or brother; and the refusing to be sworn, with a stubbornness like that of bullocks, or stones, or wood; the taking of a little bread and the juice of the grape, and asking a blessing to rest on the crown of your heads; and kneeling down upon the ground and praying, and rising from prayer with drops of water falling from your noses, and with tears rolling down from your eyes."

When we consider, in the light thus thrown upon it, the character of these Christian confessors, we can understand why it was when bonds, imprisonment, tortures, and death awaited them, that they denied nothing, concealed nothing, and feared nothing. Nor is it wonderful that

EXAMINATION OF CHRISTIANS.

others who saw their boldness took knowledge of them that they had been with Jesus. The husband of one of those who were bound at this time was so impressed with what he heard, that he came up to the prisoners and said—"Be not afraid, for it is well if for that you die." Upon this, he too was apprehended, and, having confessed his faith in Christ, was bound, and led away with the others.

Nineteen Christians now lay under sentence of death, and their brethren knew that their execution was fixed for the morrow. What could they do? Let us observe their proceedings.

The midnight hour has closed a day of terror, and yet of triumph to the Christians—one of the darkest, but one of the brightest in the history of Madagascar. Though the city is still, here and there might have been seen individuals and groups quietly leave their dwellings and steal noiselessly along the streets. Whither are they going? The word has passed from one to another that they are to meet to offer prayer for their suffering brethren. "And at one at night," writes one of those who were present, and who took part in the service, "we met together, and prayed." What meaning is there in these simple words, and what power was there in the exercise they describe! Had we listened, as these men of prayer cried, like their Saviour, with strong cryings and tears, to Him who was able to succour and to save, how assured should we have felt that such supplications would bring down Divine help to their suffering friends!

To see the proof of this, we have only to visit other spots, and gaze upon other scenes which were made memorable upon that day. The voice of prayer, as it rose from

the assembled believers, had scarcely died away, and the
light of morning had not yet appeared, when the city was
all astir. Swiftly and widely had the intelligence spread
on the previous evening, that the decree of the Queen had
gone forth, and that on the following day nineteen Christians would suffer; and great was the multitude which
now hastened to the spots where these noble martyrs would
demonstrate the sincerity of their faith in Jesus, and the
strength of their love to His cause, by following Him in the
same pathway of sorrow which He trod, and laying down
their lives for His sake.

There were two spots to be rendered almost sacred by
the sufferings and the spirit of those who were there
cruelly sacrificed upon that day. One is called ARAPIMA-
RINANA. The meaning of the name is, "the place of
hurling down." It is in the midst of the city, and the
place of execution is a precipice of granite rock, 150 feet
high, over which condemned persons were flung. Hither,
on this dreadful morning, flowed the stream of people:
some prompted by the desire of excitement, others by their
hatred to the Christians, but many, no doubt, by deep
sympathy; and here, crowding the dreadful spot almost
to the edge of the giddy precipice, stood the gathered
throng. But let us turn from them to the prison. Meek,
like their Divine Master, though seized with rude violence
and flung upon the ground, no complaint escapes the
sufferers' lips. But other sounds are heard. As they sit
upon the prison floor, with heart and voice they unite in
singing a favourite hymn, which thus begins—

   " When I shall die, and leave my friends,
    When they shall weep for me,

When departed has my life,
Then I shall happy be!"

And when that hymn was ended, they began another, the first line of which is—

" When I shall, rejoicing, behold Him in the heavens."

But these sounds of sacred melody were now drowned by the hoarse, harsh voice of the Queen's messenger, who, in the name of Ranavalona, is pronouncing upon each the sentence they were that day to suffer. Four of them were nobles, two of whom were husband and wife. As it was unlawful to shed the blood of persons of their rank, they were to be burned alive, and the remaining fifteen* to be thrown from " the place of hurling down." As the officer was leaving the prison, the nobles sent to request the Queen that they might be strangled before their bodies were burned; but even such mercy was denied. The fifteen having been wrapped in mats, and mats having been thrust into their mouths to prevent their speaking to each other, or to the people, were then hung by their hands and feet to poles, and were thus carried to the place of execution. But the attempt wholly to silence them failed, for they prayed, and addressed the crowd as they were borne along. "And some," we are told, "who beheld them, said that their faces were like the faces of angels."

Thus they reached ARAPIMARINANA. A rope was then

---

* Mr. Ellis speaks of eighteen, but the author has followed the authority of native letters written at the time, from which it appears that fourteen suffered, and one, a young female, was saved.

firmly tied round the body of each, and one by one, fourteen of them were lowered a little way over the precipice. While in this position, and when it was hoped by their persecutors that their courage would fail, the executioner, holding a knife in his hand, stood waiting for the command of the officer to cut the rope. The question was then put for the last time, " Will you cease to pray?" But only one answer was returned. It was an emphatic "No !" The signal was then made, the rope was cut, and in another moment the mangled and bleeding body lay upon the rocks below. One of these brave sufferers for Christ, whose name was Ramonambonina, as he was led to the edge of the precipice, begged his executioners to give him a short time to pray, " for on that account," he said, " I am to be killed." His request being granted, he kneeled down and prayed aloud very earnestly. Then rising up, he first addressed the people in tones and words of solemn eloquence which amazed all, and awed many; and then, turning to his executioners, he said, "My *body* you will cast down this precipice ; but my *soul* you cannot, as it will go up to heaven to God. Therefore it is gratifying to me to die in the service of my Maker."

What the people thought and said, as they left that spot and returned to their homes, we are not told, but who can doubt that from that hour not a few saw for the first time, the truth, and felt the power of the religion of Jesus ?

Mr. Ellis and the Bishop of Mauritius visited this spot, and the latter thus refers to it :—

" It was a very harrowing spectacle to witness the actual rock from which our brethren and sisters have been thrown with so much cruelty to meet so fearful a death ; but the

evidence was clear that they died with unfailing faith and triumphant hope. The brother of one of the sufferers was with us—a manly and devoted Christian he seemed to be. I saw him every day, I believe, while I was in Antananarivo, and sometimes twice a day and oftener. He brought his children to see me, and from all that I saw of him, I was led to form the highest opinion of his straightforward, earnest, Christian character ; but, when he afterwards came to the spot to which the bodies had been taken to be burnt, he wept like a child at the recollection of his brother's sufferings. One severe part of the fiery trial through which these Christians passed on to their rest with God, was their being placed where they could see the fall of their brethren, and then being asked whether they would not recant. All such attempts to move them proved ineffectual. They seemed so filled with the love of their Saviour, and with joyful hope of heaven, that they utterly despised all offers of life on such conditions. One very striking instance I heard of from an old officer of the palace, as well as from our companions on that day. A young woman who was very beautiful and accomplished, and who was very much liked by the Queen, was placed where she could see her companions fall, and was asked, at the instance of the Queen—who wished to save her life, but could not exempt her from the common sentence against the Christians—whether she would not worship the gods, and save her life. She refused, manifesting so much determination to go with her brethren and sisters to heaven, that the officer standing by struck her on the head, and said, ' You are a fool ! you are mad !' And they sent to the Queen and told her that she had lost her reason, and should be sent to some place of safe keeping. She was sent away, strongly guarded, into the country, some thirty miles, and afterwards was married to a Christian man, and died only two years ago, leaving two or three children behind her."

But there is another place where martyrs of Jesus are to suffer on this fatal day. Its name is FARAVOHITRA, which means "the last village." Let our readers mark it well. The King of Madagascar has given it, and three other spots consecrated by the blood of the martyrs, as the sites of Memorial Churches in memory of the martyrs. And here it is proposed that the Church shall be built by the Young People of Great Britain and Ireland, and that it shall proclaim to the present and to future generations of Madagascar, their reverence for those who suffered there.

Faravohitra stands high on the crest of a hill on the northern part of Antananarivo, and what took place there on this memorable day could be seen from a large part of the city. As it was well known that four of the Christian nobles were there to be burned alive, a crowd was soon collected, and the preparations for the horrid execution were eagerly watched. The stakes were firmly fixed in the earth, fuel was laid around them, and the grim executioners stood ready for their dreadful work. Instead of being carried on poles, like their humbler brethren, it would appear that these titled sufferers were allowed to walk to the place of execution. And how great, how triumphant their faith! There was no wavering, no shrinking back from the fiery ordeal. Even the Christian lady, who had peculiar reasons for dreading the flames, was raised above all weakness and

F

fear. And as they went along, they sang together a hymn, which begins with

> " When our hearts are troubled,"

and each verse of which ends with

> "Then remember us."

They reached the place, calmly gazed upon the preparations for their death, and were fastened to the stakes. Just then a bright rainbow arched the heavens, one end of which appeared to rest almost upon the spot where they were to suffer. The pile was kindled, and then, from amidst the crackling and roaring of the fire, was heard, not the sounds of pain, but of praise. That scene, and the hymn which these martyrs sung as they rose in their fiery chariot to heaven, will never be forgotten in Madagascar. But prayer followed praise. " O Lord," they were heard to cry, " receive our spirits; for Thy love to us has caused this to come to us; and lay not this sin to their charge."

" Thus," writes a witness of that wonderful and memorable scene, " they prayed, as long as they had any life. Then they died; but softly — gently. Indeed, gently was the going forth of their life, and astonished were all the people around, that beheld the burning of them there."

But while this tragic scene is being acted there is another in progress. As the cruel orders of the Queen, in hurling the fourteen martyrs from the precipice of Arapimarina, had now been obeyed, we might have supposed that even her malignity would have been fully satisfied. But no! not yet. Hastening to the spot where lie their mangled bodies, in some of which possibly life's ex-

MARTYRDOM OF FOUR MALAGASY NOBLES.

piring flame still trembled, officers seize the ropes which
hung around them, and then, followed by the rabble, with
yells and execrations, they drag them through the streets
of the city to the spot where the four nobles had suffered.
Feeding the fires afresh which had consumed those honoured
servants of Christ, body after body was flung upon the
pile, until the horrid work had been finished.

And now pause and think awhile.   Here are Heathenism
and Christianity face to face.   " Look on this picture and
on that!"   See human nature without the Gospel : see it
with !   Contrast the passions of the Queen and her agents
—their bitter malice and fiendish ferocity—with the sweet
smiles and sacred songs of the burning nobles, and ask,
Who ? what, has made them to differ ?   Their own explanation is the only one.   It is " by the grace of God."
Nothing less is sufficient; nothing more is necessary.
Lately, Mr. Ellis surveyed the place where these things
were done, and speaking of FARAVOHITRA, he thus
writes :—

" When I visited the place in company with the Bishop
of Mauritius, we stood and gazed on the prisons in the
distance, in which the sufferers had been confined, on the
place where their sentences were read over to them, and
where, as they sat together on the ground, bound with
chains, and encircled by soldiers, they sang their hymn of
praise to Christ.   We passed up the road along which,
surrounded by an excited crowd, they raised their voices
in prayer that God would remember them.   We stood by
the side of the spot—the place itself we felt to be holy
ground—on which, when fastened to the stake, they
sang—

'There is a blessed land,
Making most happy ;
Never (thence) shall rest depart,
Nor cause of sorrow come.'

"Our companions, most of whom had been spectators
on that eventful day, and one the brother of a martyr,
pointed out where the soldiers and the heathen stood
around and cried, 'Where is Jehovah now? Why does
He not come and take you away?' To which, from the
midst of the flames, the martyrs answered, 'Jehovah is
here ; He is taking us to a better place.' Our companions
also showed us the part of the road, a little distant, on
which the relatives and associates of the Christians stood,
waving their last adieus to their rejoicing friends, who
smiled, and lifted up, as far as they could, their scorched
hands, or burning fragments of dress to return the saluta-
tion. In perfect accordance with this account is the spirit
and feeling manifested by survivors when recounting their
sufferings. I have sometimes sat as if enchained to the
lips of the venerable widow or sister of a martyr, as she
has recounted with simple pathos the suffering she has
endured ; and have been overcome with wonder and admi-
ration at the marvellous power of 'the love of Christ shed
abroad in their hearts by the Holy Ghost given unto
them.' The Christians especially rejoice in the proposal
to raise, as a perpetual memorial of these events, a church
consecrated to the worship of the martyr's God and
Saviour."

In another letter, Mr. Ellis adds, "The deep emotion
with which the Pastors and others spoke on this topic was
most affecting. Some, they said, had lost fathers, others

children, some wives, others husbands, or brothers, or
sisters, whom they now rejoiced to think of as with the
spirits of just men made perfect in heaven, but whom
they and their fellow Christians would never forget. If
churches, they said, were built upon the spots on which
they had suffered and died for the love of Christ, it would
not only comfort surviving friends, but do much to perpetuate the impressions which their constancy had produced
upon the minds of both Christians and heathens."

But while, for a brief space, our earnest thought is naturally fixed upon those who, in this fiery persecution, died
for Christ, we must not overlook the far larger number who
at the same time were condemned to suffer in the same cause.
Not a few were consigned to a life of slavery. More than a
hundred of their number were flogged, and sentenced to
work in chains during their lives. Some who were also
made slaves, might purchase back their liberty and the
liberty of their wives and children, if money enough could
be found. Many were heavily fined, and those who
had been among the great and noble of the land were
stripped of their honours and titles, and even forced to the
hardest and meanest labour. Altogether, in the early
spring of 1849—that fearful year for the Christians, truly
called the year of "the great persecution"—1903 were
punished, because they had either professed or favoured
the religion of Jesus.

Some who had been officers in the army were reduced
to the rank of common soldiers; but to add to the punishment, they were ordered to build a stone house. This was
a severe task, especially for men altogether unused to such
labour, for they were compelled to go into the quarry, to

dig out the blocks of stone, and then to carry them to the site of the building. Hard-hearted taskmasters were placed over them; their clothing was bare, and their food short; but on and on they were forced to work for a whole year. And besides this, they were branded with the name, "Tsihiaharana," which means, "That which is not to be imitated," to prevent others, who witnessed their sufferings, from obeying the Gospel. Nor was this all. As soon as they had completed one heavy task, they were called to others equally laborious. Thus, after the house had been built, the same band of Christians was sent into the forest to fell large trees, and, though there were no roads, to drag them over hill and dale, to a considerable distance. Some were despatched to fight the Sakalaves, and to remain in the enemy's country during the wet season, when the deadly fever prevailed. One of these Christians thus writes:—"I was condemned to slavery, and valued at thirty dollars. My wife and children were also made slaves. My property was all taken from me. I was aide-de-camp to Rainiharo, and had been promoted to the eighth honour.* But mine honour was taken from me, and I was made a common soldier, to carry a musket, and perform the exercise of a soldier once every fortnight, until my skin peeled off, like that of a serpent, every time we performed the exercise; for we were not allowed to wear either a hat or a shirt, but only a girdle around our loins. 'Blessed be God, who lightens our sorrows." 2 Cor. v.

Amongst those who were condemned at this time, was the Prince Ramonja. Though a favourite of his aunt, he was sentenced to pay a heavy fine, and to be stripped of his

* About equal to that of a Colonel in the army.

honours.   But he suffered all with Christian meekness.
No man was more deservedly beloved and honoured by
his brethren than he.   His house became their meeting
and sometimes their hiding-place, and most cheerfully did
he expend his remaining property in providing for those
who had been robbed of their all.   " He is a wise man,"
writes one who had not only seen, but experienced his
help, " and truly loves Christ.   He fights the good fight
every day.   He preaches constantly to the Queen, though
her heart kindles against him whenever he opens his mouth
on the subject of Christianity.   *   *   He is at present
called to bear greater affliction, and to carry a heavier cross
than any of the Christians ; but he considers all this light,
and preaches the word boldly, and continually to the
Queen and to his relations.   He does not mind the rage
of his sovereign's heart against him, but we, his companions, are very sorry for what he has been called to endure.
His relations often upbraid him for what he suffers.   ' He
does not follow the religion of his ancestors, but he fol-
lows the religion of the ancestors of the white people, and
that is the reason of his afflictions.'   But the Prince speaks
to them, saying, 'I do *not* worship the ancestors of
strangers, nor my own ancestors, but God, that made
heaven and earth : Him alone do I worship ; and Jesus
Christ, who died for the sins of men.'   They consider him
on this account obstinate, but the Queen does not punish
him, because he is her sister's beloved son."

   If the fear of pain, privation, and death could have
shaken the faith and courage of the Madagascar Christians,
we should have heard little more about them after this
terrible trial.   But none of these things moved them.

They encouraged themselves and each other in the Lord, and were consoled by the conviction that the day of their deliverance would come. Secretly, therefore, but yet steadily, they travelled on in the path of duty, though it was ofttimes a way of darkness and difficulty. Fearless of consequences, they still assembled for worship. And there were now seven houses in the capital, and others in the country, where, during the dead of night, they met to consider Him whose love for them was stronger than death, and to speak and hear of that world where "the wicked cease from troubling, and the weary are at rest." In this they were countenanced by the example of the Prince Royal, of Ramonja, and of others high in rank, who were ready to lay their honours and their lives at the Saviour's feet. And after a time, a few appeared in their solemn assemblies whom they little expected to see there. These were beloved brethren who had been banished from the capital, but who had found their way back to it. Still they were " prisoners of the Lord," and in bonds. Each of them bore the heavy iron fetters that had from the first been rivetted upon their limbs ; and a strange spectacle must they have presented to the Christians as they entered their meetings, and very sad the sound of their clanking chains, as they returned the salutations of their brethren, or lifted their fettered hands to God in prayer. But doubtless such courage and constancy as they had shown, must have cheered the hearts and confirmed the faith of many who saw that though " persecuted " they were not "forsaken."

There were others at these private gatherings who had suffered the loss of all things. The imposition of fines

had left them penniless. But this only furnished occasion for
new manifestations of Christian principle and affection. It
might almost be said that, like primitive believers, they had
all things common. This, at least, is certain, that the
noble man who now reigns, his devout cousin, and others
of the more wealthy Christians, appropriated nearly all
their property in assisting their destitute brethren.

The chief cause of the wonderful firmness of these Christians was their simple faith in God's Word, their familiar
acquaintance with its contents, and the deep love with which
they regarded it. Most truly was it their meditation day
and night, the man of their counsel, sweeter than honey,
better than their necessary food, more precious than thousands of gold and silver. But that Word was scarce.
Many books had been given up, and others had been discovered by the diligent search of the Queen's officers. Only
a few were still hidden or buried; and very many were without this treasure. But these heard it read, or borrowed
it from their brethren; and in this way they richly stored
their memories with its contents. The letters written to
the Missionaries after their departure are replete with
indications of this, as scarcely a statement or a sentiment
occurs which is not supported by Scripture references.

The Directors, and their friends at Mauritius, made
repeated attempts to satisfy the cravings of the Christians
for Bibles, but the obstacles were so formidable that few
copies could be added to their scanty stock.

Describing his first visit to Tamatave, Mr. Ellis says that
nothing struck him so much as the earnest, repeated, and
importunate applications for the Scriptures, and Christian
books, which reached him from all quarters. "One fine-

looking young officer," he writes, in a letter to the Directors, " who had come from a distance, on hearing that we were at Tamatave, almost wept, when, in reply to his earnest request for a book, Mr. Cameron told him that he had not a single copy left."

While Mr. Ellis was at Mauritius, he received a letter from a Christian who had nearly lost his sight, in consequence of having devoted years in copying portions of Scripture for his Christian brethren.

One evening, while at Tamatave, two men called at Mr. Ellis's house. On being admitted, they told him that, having heard that he had brought the Bible to their land, they had come a long way in order to get a copy. As they were strangers to him, he thought that possibly they might be spies, and that, if he complied with their request, he might be banished from the island. He told them, therefore, that he could not give them what they wanted then, but that they might call upon him again on the following morning. In the meantime, he made inquiries about them from some of the Christians of the place, and learned that they were excellent men, and members of a family that feared the Lord greatly; that they lived at the capital, and having come down about a hundred and fifty miles towards the coast on business, and having there heard that Mr. Ellis was at Tamatave with the Word of God, they resolved to travel more than a hundred miles further, in the hope that they might secure this treasure for themselves. Of course Mr. Ellis was delighted to hear such a report of these worthy men, and was ready, when they called again on the following morning, to give them what they wanted. Before doing this, however, he learned from them that their family was large, and scattered, but that all of the members of it were Christians. When asked whether they had the Scriptures, they told Mr. Ellis that they had seen them, and heard them, but that all they possessed were "some of the words of David," which, however, did not belong to themselves alone, but to the whole family. He further ascertained that this sacred fragment was sent from one to another, and that each, after keeping it for a time, passed it on, until it had been read by all. Mr. Ellis then inquired whether they had these "words of David" with them. This was a question which they seemed unwilling to answer; but at length they confessed that they had. Mr. Ellis having asked to see the book, they looked at one another, and appeared as if they knew not what to do. At length one of them thrust his hand deep into his bosom, and from beneath the folds of his lamba he drew forth a parcel. This he very slowly and carefully opened. One piece of cloth after another was gently removed, when at length there appeared a few leaves of the Book of Psalms, which the good man cautiously handed to Mr. Ellis. Though it was evident that the greatest care had been taken of them, their dingy colour, their worn edges, and other marks of frequent use, showed plainly enough how much they had been read. We can only fancy the feelings with which our friend looked upon these few soiled and well-worn leaves, revealing as they did the deep love which these Christians feel for God's Word, and the diligence with which they keep and use it. Desiring to possess these precious fragments, Mr. Ellis asked the men whether they had not seen other words of David besides those which they now produced, and also the words of Jesus, and of

Paul, of Peter, and of John? "Yes," they replied, "they had seen and heard them, but they had them not." "Well, then," said Mr. Ellis, holding out the tattered leaves, "if you will give me these few words of David, I will give you *all* his words, and I will give you besides, the words of Jesus, and of John, and of Paul, and of Peter." Upon this he handed to them a copy of the New Testament and the Psalms, bound together, and said, "You shall have all these if you will give me this." The men were at first amazed. Then they compared the Psalms they had with those in the book, and having satisfied themselves that all their own words of David were in it, with many more, and that beside these there were other Scriptures which they greatly desired, light beamed in their faces, they took Mr. Ellis at his word, gave him those leaves of the Book of Psalms which had so long yielded them comfort, seized the volume he offered in exchange, bid him farewell, and hastily left the house. In the course of the day he inquired after them, wishing to speak to them again, when the Christians at Tamatave told him that, as soon as they left his house, they set out upon their long journey to the capital, doubtless "rejoicing as one that findeth great spoil."

For two or three years after the great persecution, there was a lull in the tempest. But this was not the effect of any change in the Queen's feelings towards her Christian subjects. "Her wrath," writes one of them, in 1852, "continues to rage against us, for there is a law written in a book, stating, 'That no person is allowed to pray and worship according to the religion of the white people. He that does that shall be put to death,' saith the sovereign.

'The worship and religion of my ancestors you must follow and practise for ever and ever, but the worship or religion of any other people shall never be allowed in my country,' saith the Queen. This law is read every fortnight to the soldiers, when they are exercised."

But though still "breathing out threatening and slaughter against the disciples of the Lord," her violence was at this time restrained. This, doubtless, may be ascribed in part to the influence of her son, the Prince Ramonja, and other Christian nobles, with whose assistance in the conduct of the Government she could not dispense. But the principal cause was the death of Rainiharo, her chief minister, and great favourite. From the commencement of the persecution, this hard man had been forward to advise, and execute the most severe measures against the hated Christians, and in him the Queen ever found a ready instrument of her will. But his direful career was now closed, and the Christians had a brief respite from persecution, and indulged the hope that their deliverance drew nigh. What confirmed this hope was the fact that Roharo, Rainiharo's son, who was a friend of the Prince, and now, through Rakoto's influence, commander of the forces, had joined himself to them. Nor was this all. Left without her chief minister, and feeling the effects of age and disease, the Queen from this time leaned more than ever upon her son, and, to some extent, shared the Government with him. In 1853, indeed, it was believed that she had resolved to abdicate in his favour; and this was so positively stated, that the Directors sent Messrs. Ellis and Cameron to Madagascar, to ascertain the truth, and if practicable, to

prepare for the recommencement of Missionary operation. But these hopes were not realized. Nevertheless, the intelligence obtained by Mr. Ellis, both on this
and two subsequent visits, was of the greatest value, and
such as to justify the conclusion that the time to favour
Madagascar was at hand.

Mr. Ellis's admirable volume has been so extensively
read that its contents are familiar to most. It may therefore suffice to say, that during the month he passed at the
capital on his third visit, in 1856, his intercourse with the
Christians of all classes, and the information he obtained
from them, proved to be of inestimable value. Much came
under his notice to show their steadfastness and their increase; and although no change had passed over the spirit
of the Queen, there appeared good reason for the hope
that severe measures against the Christians would not be
renewed.

But these calculations proved to be unfounded. Another time of great trouble was at hand—as great as any
that had preceded it. The full particulars of this persecution have not as yet been received, but the following brief
statement will indicate its origin and its consequences.

For some years there had been some French residents at
Antananarivo, who, by their mechanical knowledge and mer-
cantile transactions, had made themselves useful to the Government. One of these had resided there for several years.
Under the pretext of delivering the country from the cruel-
ties and oppression of Ranavalona, these men determined,
if possible, to dethrone her, and to establish a "French Pro-
tectorate"—that false and fraudulent misnomer for French
usurpation. By their promises and persuasions they had

gained over several men of rank and influence, and had also
secreted in one of their own houses a large quantity of arms,
armour, and ammunition. Everything having been arranged,
the night was fixed upon in which the palace was to be invaded, the Queen seized, and the new Government proclaimed. But Ranavalona heard of the plot, confined the
conspirators, and finally sentenced them to perpetual banishment from the country. Amongst the party there was a
Catholic lady and two Jesuit priests. The latter, disguised
as an apothecary and a physician's assistant, were met by
Mr. Ellis on his return from Antananarivo. The so-called
" assistant," however, proved to be the Abbé Jouan, the
principal of a Jesuit college at Bourbon. Such shameless
pretenders were meet companions for reckless conspirators.

Had the frustration of the plot and the banishment of
its authors been the sole results of its discovery, it would
not have been noticed here. But, unhappily, while the
guilty escaped, the innocent suffered. How far any of the
Christians, groaning under cruel oppression, and expecting
deliverance from the proposed change in the Government,
were drawn into the snare, is not known. But it was sufficient for the Queen that Christians were still amongst
her subjects, notwithstanding her edicts, her punishments, and her threats. She resolved, therefore, that,
whether guilty or not, they should suffer for that which
strangers had devised, and of which the great multitude
had not even heard. Like the sudden eruption of the long
pent-up fires of a volcano, the wrath of the Queen once
more burst forth with desolating fury.

The 3rd of July was one of those awful days of doom,
of which the Christians of Antananarivo had seen but too

many during the present reign. Early in the morning of
that day, the announcement was made by the Queen's
officers that a great kabary was to be held. What this
foreboded they knew but too well: and they did not
conceal their fears; for, together with the royal summons came the intelligence that they were hemmed in by
soldiers stationed at every outlet of the city, so that escape
was impossible. At the same time, officers broke into
their houses, and forcibly drove them to the place of the
great assembly.

"There was," said an eye-witness, "a general howling
and wailing, a rushing and running through the streets,
as if the town had been attacked by a hostile army."
At length the appointed hour came. Within the great
square, thousands of people, strongly guarded, were
crowded together, many of them waiting with dread the
announcement of the royal pleasure. At length, a Queen's
messenger, with a loud voice delivered the following message from his dreaded mistress :—That she had long suspected that there were many Christians still amongst
her people, and that, within the last few days, she had
discovered that several thousands of them dwelt in and
around her capital;—that every one knew how she hated
this sect, and how strictly she had forbidden the practice
of their religion;—that she should do her utmost to
discover the guilty, and would punish them with the
greatest severity; and that all should die who did not,
within fifteen days, submit themselves to her pleasure.

What added to the danger of the Christians was the
circumstance that one of their worst foes had in his pos-
session a list of the names of all who dwelt in the city,

which he intended to send to the Queen. For this purpose he commissioned one of her attendants to deliver it; but, providentially, this man, who was a firm friend of the Prince, and favourable to the Christians, brought the document to him. He read it, and the next moment tore it into fragments and scattered it about the ground. This bold but prudent act saved many, most probably hundreds, of lives; and as the accused were now warned, numbers of them, as soon as they could find an egress from the city, either fled to the forests, or by other means escaped the fury of the storm. But all were not so fortunate. Some were seized and put to the torture, that they might be forced to disclose the names of their brethren; and while this was going on, every house was entered by soldiers, and every person suspected of Christianity was consigned to prison. One of the prisons used on that occasion had originally been a chapel, and to that sacred purpose it has now been restored by Radama II. But at the time of which we write, many Christians were crowded there and cruelly tormented, by a royal order.

What a contrast the scenes then witnessed, the sufferings then endured, and the dangers then impending, presents to the congregations who now, under the same roof, listen to God's Word, and with the voice of joy and melody sing forth the honour of His name! We can readily believe what Mr. Ellis states, that "the people have almost as strong an attachment to this scene of their distress and sorrow, as to the spots on which their companions actually died."

Six days after her decree, the Queen heard that com-

paratively few Christians had been apprehended. This made
her more furious than ever. Her rage indeed seemed to
know no bounds. "The bowels of the earth," she said,
"shall be searched, and the rivers and lakes shall be
dragged with nets, rather than that one Christian shall
escape." At the same time, new orders to track them to
their hiding-places were issued to the officers and soldiers
of her army; and another kabary was held, when it was
proclaimed that whoever helped, or did not hinder their
escape, should surely die. But these violent measures
were to a large extent in vain. The entire population of
one village, nine miles from the capital, was thus saved
from death. Fifteen hundred soldiers were sent to surprise the place and secure the victims; but happily, on
their arrival, all the inhabitants had fled.

The first victim of this cruel outburst of the insensate
despot was an aged Christian female, who, before the nine
days given for self-accusation, was dragged away to the
market-place, and, horrible to relate, her backbone was
sawn asunder. This was on the 11th of July; but the
next morning, six more Christians were taken at a village
not far from the city. Their concealment, however, had
been so contrived as very nearly to have prevented their
discovery; for the soldiers had searched the hut in which
they were, and were just leaving it, when one of them said
that he had heard a cough. They therefore renewed
their search, and soon, beneath some straw, they discovered
a large hole, in which the hunted Christians were hid.
With violence they were dragged out, bound, and hurried
away to their doom. But here, unhappily, the consequences
of this discovery were not to end. The other inhabitants

of the village had been privy to the concealment of their
neighbours, and although aware of the threatened penalty,
had kept their secret, even at the risk of their own lives.
Whether they themselves, or any of them, were believers in
the Gospel is not known; but whatever might have been
its cause, their generosity met with a sad requital. The
officer in command was a stern man; he therefore ordered
his soldiers to seize every inhabitant of the place, to
bind them, and to lead them away to their fate, with the
six Christians whom they had sought to save.

It was said by those who saw her, that the Queen had
never before given way to such outbursts of rage as now;
and that at no former periods had she manifested such a
determination to exterminate the Christians. In the city,
and the surrounding villages, kabaries were held almost
daily, for the purpose of denouncing them as the cause of
all the evils which afflicted the land, and of declaring the
Queen's purpose not to rest until the last of this hated
sect had been destroyed; and, had not the register of
their names fallen into the hands of the Prince, there is
too much reason to fear that his mother's sanguinary desires would have been largely gratified. But this was not
the only aid which the watchful kindness of their friend
and protector, together with the secret but earnest efforts
of some Christian nobles who acted with him, now rendered
to the oppressed. The escape of many who had even been
apprehended, must be attributed to them. This was the
case with several of the villagers who had connived at the
concealment of their Christian neighbours, as well as
others. The marvel and the great mercy was that the
Prince himself escaped; but his savage mother seemed dead

to every human feeling save one—the love of her son. It was this natural instinct which God overruled for the preservation of Radama's own life, and through him of the lives of so many of His servants.

But notwithstanding these interpositions, human and Divine, not a few were at this period added to the number of Christian martyrs. Only fifteen days after the great kabary, ten were publicly executed, and their death was accompanied with frightful tortures. On their way to the place of execution, the soldiers goaded them on with their spears, and the blood-stained path through which they had been driven showed with what effect the weapons had been used. For what special reason is unknown, but it was ordered that they and others, to the number, it is believed, of twenty-one, should not be executed in any of the accustomed modes. It is probable, however, that as the previous martyrdom of Christians had failed to accomplish the object of their persecutors, the Queen resolved to try the effect of a more painful method. They were therefore sentenced to be stoned, but not to death; for, ere life was extinct, or consciousness lost, their heads were to be severed from their mutilated bodies, and held up to the view of the multitude. But the spirit which had sustained Stephen, and so many of their brethren who had laid down their lives for the sake of the Lord Jesus, characterized these noble sufferers. Theirs was the same unwavering faith, the same patient suffering, the same victorious death. No faltering, no timid clinging to life, no compromise with conviction, cast the faintest shadow upon the worthy name they bore, or the holy cause for which they died. As they were led out from the prison, amongst the sounds which first caught the ear was the voice of praise; and still, as they approached the fatal spot, notwithstanding the piercing of the spears, and even when crushed beneath the stones, they were happy, and almost jubilant. To quote the brief, but expressive words of a native witness of the scene, "They continued to sing hymns till they died."

These were the last of the long line of Madagascar martyrs; and most worthy successors they were of those who, through much tribulation, had entered before them into the Kingdom of God.

We have now written the closing record of the wrongs and sufferings of the faithful and much enduring Christians of Madagascar. The persecution just described was almost immediately to be followed by the day of deliverance. The cry from beneath the altar had been heard; the rod of the oppressor was broken, and a future full of high and holy promise has opened, which calls aloud for all the works of faith, the labours of love, and the patience of hope, which the servants of God can consecrate to the evangelization of that noble land. But we must now briefly sketch the features of this great change, which will form a fit and bright closing page of this eventful history.

Ranavalona, the Queen of Madagascar, was now of advanced age. Her reign had extended to thirty-three years. But the day of her death drew near. For several weeks during the summer of 1861 her strength rapidly failed, and dangerous symptoms appeared. Early in August, it was generally known that her sceptre would speedily pass into other hands. But who would possess it? This was *the* question with the people, and it was asked earnestly, anxiously, by tens of thousands. Had the decision been theirs, the issue would not have been doubtful—their warm and almost unanimous response would have been Rakoto-radama. Long had he been their hope and their desire, and throughout the land, no man was so honoured, trusted, and beloved as he. For years he had stood between the oppressor and the oppressed, and in instances without number, contrary to his mother's law, and at the peril of his own life, he had rescued the victims of her wrath from chains, from slavery, and from death. For years, the interests of his country and the highest welfare of its inhabitants had been the object of his intense solicitude; but, while the benefactor of all classes, he had been the especial friend and protector of the Christians. It was not surprising, therefore, that his accession to the throne should have been regarded with bright hopes and eager desire. But pitfalls and perils lay in his path. The Prince had a rival in his cousin Rambosalama, the son of the Queen's sister, and brother of his own wife. Older than himself, this man had been named by the Queen, at the commencement of her reign, as her successor; but when the unexpected birth of a son gave a rightful heir to the throne of Madagascar, Rambosalama lost his title. Nevertheless, he resolved, if possible, to secure the object of his ambition. Nor was he without the hope of success. Resolute, contriving, and unscrupulous, he had gained over to his side the Queen's chief adviser, Rainijoary, and many who stood near the throne; while with herself, whom he too closely resembled in his hatred of the Christians, he was a great favourite. It was confidently reported, and commonly believed, that this un-

principled man had hired assassins to remove the only
obstacle to the attainment of power, and that more than
once these wretched men had confessed to the Prince their
meditated crime. Be this as it may, it is certain that
Rakoto and his friends well knew the purpose, and
probably the plots of his rival. Amongst those in whom
he placed entire confidence, was his long-tried Christian
associate, the commander of the forces. This man, who
had attained the highest honour (the 15th) which the
Queen could confer, and more absolute power, as the head
of the army, than any other of her subjects, was, as our
readers may remember, the son of Rainiharo, so long prime
minister, and the fierce persecutor of the Christians. The
second officer in command was also one of the Prince's
warm supporters. Nevertheless, it required all their vigilance and skill to frustrate the purpose of Rambosalama
and his co-conspirators.

Within about a month of the Queen's death, the Prince
and his friends agreed that the time had come when it
behoved them to adopt measures for their own protection.
In most cases, we know what those measures would have
been,—the chain, the dungeon, and the dagger. But Rakoto,
always remarkable for his humanity, had resolved not to
pass to power over the fallen and the dead. His sole
purpose was to preserve, not to punish—to save his own
life, not to sacrifice that of others; and all his plans at
this period were governed by this purpose. But to prevent
surprise, and to be fully prepared for the coming change, he
and his advisers often met in council, that, when the
necessity arose, they might act with concord, promptitude,
and decision.

At length, at dawn of day on the 16th of August, the intelligence spread through the city that the Queen was stricken with death, and that, in a few hours, all would be over. Soon, an immense crowd filled every avenue to the palace, and was even pressing within the courts. For what purpose were they come? Had you marked the features of some of them, watched their secret and suspicious movements, and noticed the deadly weapons which they vainly attempted to conceal, their design would have been but too plainly disclosed. These were the partizans of Rambosalama; they had been brought there, that, at a given signal from him, they might cut his pathway to the vacant throne. But while the son was weeping at the death-bed of his mother, the faithful commander of the forces had his keen eye fixed full upon every movement of her would-be successor. He knew his plans and his partizans; watched his movements within the palace, and followed him out from the chamber of death, as he hastened to give the concerted signal to his ready instruments, who were waiting without. But on his way, and ere he could effect his purpose, he was seized, and hurried back in safe custody. Almost at the same instant a trumpet sounded, and more than a thousand soldiers, who were awaiting this summons, marched in strong array, and with quickened steps, to the palace.

Rakoto was now safe : his foes had been foiled, and his rival a prisoner. Soon the commander-in-chief appeared upon the balcony of the palace to announce the Queen's death, and to proclaim Radama II. as King of Madagascar. In a moment, loud shouts and wild demonstrations of joy broke forth from the soldiers and multitude, which soon

spread through the capital. For a time the people seemed
almost mad with delight, and when, towards the afternoon
of the day it was rumoured that Radama would present
himself to his subjects, every approach to the palace was
again thronged. About four o'clock, arrayed in the robes
of royalty, with the crown upon his head, and surrounded
by his chief nobles, the King appeared. It was long ere
the shouts and cries of the people could be hushed; but as
soon as silence was obtained, in a few expressive words he
begged them to be calm, and then assured them (and never,
we believe, were words more truthful) that, in becoming
their sovereign, his one desire was to devote himself to their
welfare, and to that of the country over which he reigned.

Meanwhile, Rambosalama was conducted under a strong
guard to the centre of the city, where he was compelled to
take the oath of allegiance to his cousin. After this, he was
conveyed to a residence of his own in the country, there to be
detained a prisoner, guarded by two hundred soldiers. But
this was the extent of his punishment. Not a fetter
bound his limbs, not a fraction of his large wealth was
forfeited, nor was he forbidden to communicate with his
friends. Such was the generosity, the magnanimity—we
cannot term it justice—with which the King treated the
man who had conspired against his title and his life.

The revolution thus brought about soon made itself felt.
"The sun," writes Mr. Ellis, "did not set on the day on
which Radama II. became King of Madagascar before he
had proclaimed equal protection to all its inhabitants, and
declared that every man was free to worship God according
to the dictates of his own conscience, without fear or
danger. He sent his officers to open the prison doors, to

PALACE AT ANTANANARIVO.

knock off the fetters from those to whom the joyous shouts
of the multitude without had already announced that the
day of their deliverance was come. He despatched others to
recall the remnant of the condemned ones from the remote
and pestilential districts to which they had been banished,
and where numbers had died from disease, or exhaustion
from the rude and heavy bars of iron with which they had
been chained from neck to neck together. The exiles
hastened home; men and women, worn and wasted with
suffering and want, reappeared in the city, to the astonishment of their neighbours—who had deemed them long since
dead—but to the grateful joy of their friends. The long-
desired jubilee had come, and gladness and rejoicing everywhere prevailed; for many who were not believers in the
Gospel, sympathized with the Christians in their sufferings, and rejoiced in their deliverance."

Thus, seven of these restored exiles speak of themselves
and others : " On Thursday, 29th of August, 1861, we
that were in concealment appeared. Then all the people
were astonished, when they saw us, that we were alive, and
not yet buried or eaten by the dogs; and there were a
great many of the people desiring to see us, for they considered us as dead ; and this is what astonished them. On
the 9th of September, those that were in fetters came to
Antananarivo ; but they could not walk, on account of the
weight of their heavy fetters, and their weak and feeble
bodies."

To pass over other proceedings which show how much
the King desired the social and political prosperity of the
country, it must not be forgotten that one of his earliest
acts was to lay the foundation of a large stone building as

a college, and to restore the schools throughout the country, which had been closed by his mother. He also abolished the tangena, divination, and sorcery; removed all idols from the palace and the capital, and withdrew support from them elsewhere.

While Radama II. was thus showing that God had given to him what He gave to Solomon, "largeness of heart," the Christians improved their long-lost privileges. No longer gathering together by stealth in secret places, or at the midnight hour, they now met in the very heart of the city, in buildings which their own sovereign had set apart for Divine service, and in the broad face of day; while "their unquenchable thirst after instruction," their "industry in acquiring knowledge," "the vitality and strength of the faith by which they have been sustained," "their activity and force of character," "their clear perceptions of the saving truths of the Gospel," "their family religion," their "large congregations in the city," and "the smaller assemblies in almost every village in the surrounding country," together with "the great influence for good which the sufferers of Christ exercise over their brethren by the simple, humble recital of their sufferings, always given with devout acknowledgment and thanks for the Divine consolation they received, may well encourage the most sanguine hopes for the future."*

Together with the intelligence of the Queen's death, letters reached this country which made it plain to the Directors that Missionaries, so long excluded from Madagascar, would now receive, both from the King and from

* Letter from Rev. W. Ellis.

the people, a cordial welcome. Six weeks after this great change, four of the native pastors in the capital thus write:—"We are filled with joy that the kingdom of God gains ground, and establishes itself more and more in our country. We have begun to meet for public worship at Antananarivo since Lord's-day, 29th September last. As one house was not large enough to contain us all, we had to meet in eleven separate houses, and they were all crowded to excess. When the people saw how great was the number of Christians, they were exceedingly amazed; and what increased their astonishment was the appearing in public of Christians who, having been hidden for so long a period, were considered by all as dead. Everybody could not but exclaim, 'Truly, God is great, who can thus watch over those who place their confidence in Him!' A general disposition to join us seems to take hold of the people. * * The King, Radama II., tells us to write, and persuade the Missionaries to come and settle at Antananarivo, as well as our friends and countrymen who are at Mauritius. There is now no obstacle; the way is open to everybody."

Referring to one of the congregations which he saw at the capital, the Bishop of Mauritius, says, " Mr. Ellis, who was with me, said there must have been at least 1500 persons present. I never saw anything like the fervour I there witnessed. I shortly afterwards again addressed the people, when from 1000 to 1400 persons were present, a mighty crowd pressing us in upon all sides. While I addressed them, a kind of electric feeling seemed to possess and pervade the whole assembly. I spoke to them of the fulness of the blessing of the Gospel of Christ. The

Rev. Mr. Ellis interpreted my observations, and their effect
so gratified me, that I recalled those lines of Dr. Watts,

> ' In holy duties let the day
> In holy pleasures pass away!'

* * Mr. Ellis commences his services early, and concludes
them at 11 A. M. To see the people swarm along the
streets, produces much the effect of a swarm of bees
around a bee-hive.''

To the London Missionary Society belongs the great
honour of being not only the first, but the only Protestant
Society whose agents have laboured in Madagascar. The
Embassy sent by the British Government to congratulate
Radama II. on his accession to the throne, when referring
to the cordiality with which Englishmen were welcomed to
the capital, truly remark in their official report of the visit,
" We need not look far for an explanation of this feeling.
The Missionary work initiated thirty* years ago, will sufficiently account for it. Nearly all the arts with which the
people were acquainted, were taught them by the Missionaries."

Under these circumstances, the Directors and friends of
the London Missionary Society felt that upon them the
solemn obligation peculiarly devolved of re-occupying this
field as soon as the way into it was open. The King of
Madagascar was well aware of their purpose, and therefore,
immediately after ascending the throne, his principal Secretary of State was instructed to invite the Rev. J. Le Brun,
the Society's Missionary at Mauritius, to visit the capital
without delay. Too aged to undertake the toilsome journey,

---

* It should have been "forty."

Mr. Le Brun deputed his son—accompanied by David Johns, one of the refugees, and long an evangelist to his countrymen in the Mauritius—to undertake the service.   As soon as this intelligence reached the Directors, they lost no time in making arrangements for the resumption of their labours in a land so long the object of their solicitude and their prayers, and where

ENTRANCE TO THE HARBOUR OF PORT LOUIS, MAURITIUS.

so much had been done and suffered for Christ.   But while these preparations were in progress, on the 20th of November, 1861, at their request Mr. Ellis sailed on his fourth visit to Madagascar; and on the 15th of April, 1862, he was followed by six Missionaries, including a doctor of medicine, a superintendent of schools, and a printer.

Since the departure of those brethren, almost every mail
has brought the Directors such reports from Madagascar,
as have filled their hearts with devout gratitude and gladness. From Mr. Le Brun they learned that before reaching Antananarivo, he received a letter of welcome in the
King's name, announcing that His Majesty had appropriated a house for his use, and had sent officers to conduct him to it. The day after his arrival was the Sabbath,
but it was not to him a season of rest. At an early hour
his house was invaded by Christian friends, and from
nine o'clock until two he was led from one congregation to
another, that he might, though in an unknown tongue, and
by an interpreter, utter some words of prayer to God, and
exhortation to the people. During that single morning
he took part in the services at five sanctuaries. "Where-
ever I went," he writes, " I was saluted with tears and
expressions of joy ; and whenever I pronounced the blessed
name of Jesus Christ, it was truly affecting to witness the
utterance of deep emotion by which they testified their
faith and gratitude."

Mr. Le Brun's active engagements in the capital
were terminated by illness shortly after his arrival there.
But this visit elicited many demonstrations of sympathy
and solicitude on the part of the Christians. "Day
after day, night after night, it was the same loving care,
mingled with prayer and supplication. Oh ! how fervently
did they pray as they kneeled by the side of my couch !
What tears of fraternal love and Christian sympathy they
shed, as they administered medicines, and watched with
anxiety their effect upon me !"

But though his opportunities of observation and inter-

H

course were thus restricted, Mr. Le Brun had a most
cheering audience of the King, a solemn conference with
the pastors, thrilling recitals from the lips of returned
exiles, of their dangers and deliverances, and proofs which
amazed him of the large number and rapid increase of
believers. And though weak in body, he left that place
refreshed and strengthened by all that he had there seen
and heard.

As soon as the season permitted, Mr. Ellis left Mauritius for Tamatave, where he arrived towards the end of
May. As he stepped on shore, an officer of the King's
household, who had been specially sent from the capital
for that purpose, welcomed him to Madagascar in his
royal master's name, and stated that he was commissioned
to escort him thither. The officer then presented to Mr.
Ellis a letter from Radama, expressing his desire to see
him. The same letter announced the death of Rambosalama, and thus relieved the fears which Mr. Ellis felt for
the life of the King. After this reception, he was conducted,
by a procession of chiefs and officers, to the King's house,
which a large number of native workmen had been preparing
for his temporary residence. The next morning, however,
he became the guest of the chief judge of Tamatave, where
he was honoured with presents, and treated with the utmost
kindness and consideration.

On the following day, the Christians held a thanksgiving service, at which "a goodly number was present,"
and "many seemed deeply moved." "You cannot imagine," writes Mr. Ellis, "the sensation my arrival has
occasioned, and the satisfaction I derive from all I see and
hear about the Christians."

After Mr. Ellis had been a week at Tamatave, a special messenger from the King arrived to hasten his departure for the capital. Accordingly, he left early the next morning (May 31), and on the 16th of June he reached his destination. When within thirty miles of Antananarivo, he was met by a large number of Christians from that city, with two of their pastors; but instead of expressing their joy by ordinary salutations, they came towards him with the voice of thanksgiving and melody. No reception could have been more cordial or more touching; and tears, he tells us, were the only response he could make to the devout gladness of his friends. This real *Te Deum* ended, the pastors announced that they had been sent by their brethren and the churches to bid him welcome, to assure him of their delight, and to accompany him to the capital.

Ten miles further on they rested for the Sabbath Day, at a village called Ambotomanga. It was a high day to Mr. Ellis. As he saw the chief room of the largest house in the place, " thronged with simple and devout worshippers, while numbers crowded around on the outside," he was affected on thinking of the change thus indicated in the circumstances of the Christians since his former visit in 1854. Then, when tarrying for a Sabbath in the same place, only a *few* Christians dared to meet him for prayer, and they came by stealth and at night.

Next morning, letters of welcome from the King and the principal Secretary of State were put into his hands, and soon after nine o'clock the party, consisting of about two hundred persons, set out for the capital. As they approached the city, and all through the suburbs, a warm reception was awaiting him from the gathered multitudes.

On the following day he was most cordially received by the King and Queen at the palace, in the presence of the nobles of the Court, who expressed their great gratification at the expression of friendship on the part of the English, and the endeavours of the London Missionary Society to impart to his people the blessings of Christianity and education.

During the next week, Mr. Ellis's house was thronged with Christian friends, not merely with those who resided in the capital, but with others from distant parts of the country. The only drawback to his joy was the disappointment which many evinced when told that he had not brought with him what they longed to possess—copies of God's Word. On the two following Sabbaths he attended two of their places of worship, which consisted of houses with the partitions and fronts removed, to afford sufficient accommodation. Each of these rude sanctuaries was, with an interval of two hours, densely filled, from daybreak to five o'clock, with congregations of about 1500. " No description," Mr. Ellis writes, " can convey to you any correct idea of the seriousness, attention, apparent devotion, and deep feeling of these assemblies during the time of worship."

We cannot, and indeed need not follow Mr. Ellis through the details of his almost incessant occupations. The subjoined extracts will sufficiently show their number, interest, and importance.

" I am occasionally sent for by the King or some of the high officers, and I have for some short time past attended His Majesty at his house daily, from one to three o'clock, to read English with him. We read together out of a large quarto Bible, on the outside of which is inscribed in gilt

THE KING AND QUEEN OF MADAGASCAR.

letters, "Presented to Radama, King of Madagascar, by
the London Missionary Society, 1821.' A number of
officers, some of them Christians, are generally present,
and we frequently converse on what we have read. I have
also every forenoon at my house, eleven or twelve sons of
the chief nobles and officers, who come to learn English
an hour and a half daily. They will be the future rulers
of the country. They accompany me to the chapel, and
sometimes to my readings with the King. Last Sunday,
with His Majesty's approval, I held Divine service at the
King's house at three o'clock in the afternoon; His Majesty,
some of his high officers, all my pupils, and a number of
others, were present. I read in the Old and New Testament; we sang twice; when I prayed, partly in English,
and partly in Malagasy, concluding with the Lord's
Prayer in Malagasy. Then I occupied about a quarter
of an hour in an address from 1 Tim. i. 15 : 'This is a
faithful saying, and worthy of all acceptation, that Christ
Jesus came into the world to save sinners.' This was
faithfully translated by Ra Haniraka. All were very
attentive. I was informed that the King expressed his
approval, and I hope to be permitted to continue the
service. I have seen nothing yet to diminish the high
opinion I had formed of the strength and purity of the
religious feeling among the people. I attend the King
daily, read the Scriptures with him, and converse with
him on their contents as well as on other matters. I continue my Sunday service at his house, and, as I am told
by his officers, with increasing interest and satisfaction to
the King, who sometimes interrupts me to express his
entire concurrence in something I may have said, or to

impress it more forcibly upon the minds of the hearers.
Besides these engagements—which take the best hours of
every day, viz., from half-past ten in the morning till three
in the afternoon—my house, during other intervals, is
seldom free from persons who come to seek medical aid,
or instruction and advice on religious subjects."

As a further illustration of the devout character of the
Christians in Madagascar, the following extract, from a
speech of the Bishop of Mauritius, may be added.

" One evening I was obliged from fatigue to go into my
cot, and fell asleep. I was awakened in the early morning
by the voices of persons who were engaged in reading the
Scriptures, and prayer, and on inquiry I was informed that
these exercises had been carried on throughout the night.
* * * They were ever ready for prayer and reading
the Scriptures—more so, indeed, than I was able at all
times to assist in, owing to my being sick with fever.

" In testimony of their desire to read and hear the Word
of God, I now hold in my hand a copy of the New Testament, which, when I left Mauritius, was quite strong and
all but new. I was only a few weeks in Madagascar ; but
such was the desire of the people to handle the sacred
volume, that my copy of it has been reduced to the state
to which frequent use of it by them now exhibits it to
you. All these young men were able to read ; and one of
them engaged in prayer. This was precisely the state of
things I met with throughout my passage from the coast
to the capital. In the capital and its immediate neighbourhood I was struck by yet more sterling proofs of the
abiding power of God's Word. * * * I met with
many Christians who appeared to have had the truth brought

to their knowledge in a very special and striking manner. Some of these I particularly questioned. One of them had been taught Christianity by a Hova mother. She had been seized, imprisoned, and had almost miraculously escaped. Seized again, she was again imprisoned, and put to death, with horrible torture. * * * With reference to the way in which the Bible has been circulated, and its knowledge spread abroad in Madagascar, I will only mention one further instance. A young man possessed a Bible, which he had invariably carried about his person during a period of eighteen years. In the course of that time his Bible had frequently been exposed to destruction; but he had dwelt with peculiar confidence and satisfaction upon that passage in Jeremiah, ' But fear not thou, O my servant Jacob, and be not dismayed, O Israel; for behold ! I will save thee from afar off, and thy seed from the land of their captivity; and Jacob shall return and be in rest and at ease, and none shall make him afraid.' That poor man had read this in the midst of his troubles, and he was not afraid. He went on his way; and here, he said to me, we are now in good health and in safety. He further quoted to me the 11th and 12th verses of the same book, ' Be not afraid,' &c., and six other similar passages."

The most recent communications convey the intelligence that the Missionary band has been welcomed at Antananarivo, and are assiduously applying themselves to the acquisition of the language, and rendering their best assistance in promoting the objects of their Mission. The services of Dr. Davidson, the Medical Missionary, were in great request. All classes appreciated his skill and kindness. His patients numbered about two hundred and fifty daily.

Although the preceding pages contain numerous illustrations of the trial and the triumph of the faith of many
in bonds, imprisonment, exile, slavery, torture, and death,
and at the same time prove that persecution did not prevent, but rather promoted the cause it was designed
to destroy, it must have been evident to every thoughtful
reader that large additions were yet to be made to such
records, and fresh evidence brought to light of the prevalence
and power of the Gospel.

It will also have been noticed, as we have traced the history
of the late Queen's reign, that many of her Christian subjects were condemned to life-long slavery, and that others had
effected their escape, and were either at a safe distance from
the capital, or evading, in the forest, or other hiding-place,
the active search of their foes.   Many of these have passed
away, in exile and sorrow, in solitude or amongst strangers,
to their rest in heaven.   *Their* record is on high ; probably,
no page on earth will ever contain it.   But this is not the
case with all.   Some survive, and to them, as we have seen,
the accession of Radama II. has been the year of jubilee.
They have returned from their long captivity.   And now the
events of their lives and the fruits of their labours are beginning to be known.   It is the singular privilege of Mr.
Ellis to hear their own thrilling histories from the lips of
these faithful brethren.   Seldom does he preach without
seeing some of them amongst his hearers, and occasionally,
two or three come to his residence in the evening with
their relatives, and with one of the native pastors, and remain
for family worship.   Amongst these are individuals who had
long worn heavy fetters—fetters now happily struck off

from their limbs, and on their way to the Missionary Museum in Blomfield Street. One of these relics of the late reign of terror is an iron ring, which was worn around her ankle by an eminent Christian woman, the wife of a native pastor, who died in her chains rather than deny the Lord who bought her. During the persecution, her husband was one of the most earnest and efficient preachers. But he was able to conceal himself until the storm was overpast, when he reappeared amongst his brethren, and has resumed the work to which God had called him. " The more," writes Mr. Ellis, " I see of these Christians, the more I admire and praise God for their patient endurance and humble triumph."

" I was shown," says the Bishop of Mauritius, " a chain, although the person who showed it to me had previously stated that he ' did not like' to exhibit it. It consisted of very heavy iron rings—now broken and cut through—and had been for many long years around the ankles of a poor Christian woman, whose life those rings had helped to wear away ! Other instruments of torture— one of them a long iron bar with adjusting rings—were shown to me by a person who bore marks of the suffering these had occasioned, but must carry those marks to his grave ; but in spite of this, the Word of God has yet gone on and prevailed."

But the most interesting and important of the communications which have reached the capital since the Queen's death are from remote parts of the island. One of these is 200 miles distant. Thither some of the Christians who suffered during the early period of persecution were banished. But they carried with them the precious truths for the faith and love of which they suffered. Yet, though they were enslaved, "the Word of God was not bound." "But in the fulness of their hearts, their mouths spoke of Christ and His salvation. What has been the result? A wide and glorious harvest," writes Mr. Ellis, "invites the reapers to the field. * * *I am informed that there are thousands of believers in the Belsileo country.* Nor is this the only remote region, in which fruits of Christian effort have sprung up during the darkness which has now passed away. In a postscript to a letter which arrived while these sheets were passing through the press, occur the following pregnant and suggestive words. " I received a visit from another party of Christians far to the south on the east coast. *The Hova officers at the military post have been the evangelists.*"

Such "marvellous and gratifying" revelations of the previously unknown and unanticipated effects of Christian influence in the more remote parts of Madagascar, concurring with the fact that in the capital the " numbers continue to increase," justify large expectations. But still the friends of Missions should rejoice with trembling. One period of great trial has indeed passed, but another may be at hand. Prosperity may prove more fatal than persecution—the sunshine than the storm.

> " E'en more the treach'rous calm we dread,
> Than tempests bursting o'er our head."

But, added to the enervating influences to which too frequently Christians have yielded when "rest" has been obtained "from adversity," there are active agencies at work which must be met with vigilance and energy. It is well known that as soon as the country was open, large numbers of Catholic priests hastened to the capital. These enemies of the truth will do their utmost to sow tares amongst the wheat; and the friends of Protestant Christianity must labour earnestly to counteract their influence. Thus, with God's blessing, mischief will be prevented. Happily, the Bible was in Madagascar before the priest, and that blessed book, when read and pondered, loved and preached, as it is by the Malagasy, is mighty through God against the subtleties and sophistries of Rome. The testimony, therefore, of Father Jouen, that "the whole Christianity" of the Malagasy "consists in reading the Bible," rightly interpreted, is fraught with high encouragement. We expect great things, therefore, in the future, and this expectation is confirmed by the fact that those who would beguile the people begin to despair of success. Many of the priests have already left the capital, and the Bishop of Mauritius makes the following important statement upon the subject :—

"My firm impression is, that it is not of the least use to attempt to spread the Roman Catholic religion in Madagascar. One of the Roman Catholic priests, whom I met there, observed to me that one might just as well attempt *to cut a rock with a razor* as attempt to make Roman Catholics of the Malagasy."

But, that this and other evils may be prevented, we must pray without ceasing. And if prayers such as have prevailed on behalf of the persecuted, be presented with the same faith and fervour on behalf of the prosperous, their "power with God" will be as manifest in the one case, as in the other. But with prayer there must be a large increase of Christian labour. God has signally honoured the London Missionary Society, in permitting it to commence so great a work in Madagascar. But the Directors of that Institution feel that together with the honour there is a weighty obligation to carry it on with an energy, and upon a scale in some degree commensurate with the wide extent of the field to be cultivated, and with the assurance, founded upon the past and the present, that the time is at hand when, with the blessing of Him who is "Head over all," that noble island will be filled with the knowledge of His salvation, and sustain a position and exert an influence which will entitle it to even a more honourable name than "The Great Britain of Africa."

William Stevens, Printer, 37, Bell Yard, Temple Bar.

www.ingramcontent.com/pod-product-compliance
Lightning Source LLC
Chambersburg PA
CBHW030622270326
41927CB00007B/1285